GOING
HOLLYWOOD

Also by Josh Becker

The Complete Guide to Low-Budget Feature Filmmaking
Rushes

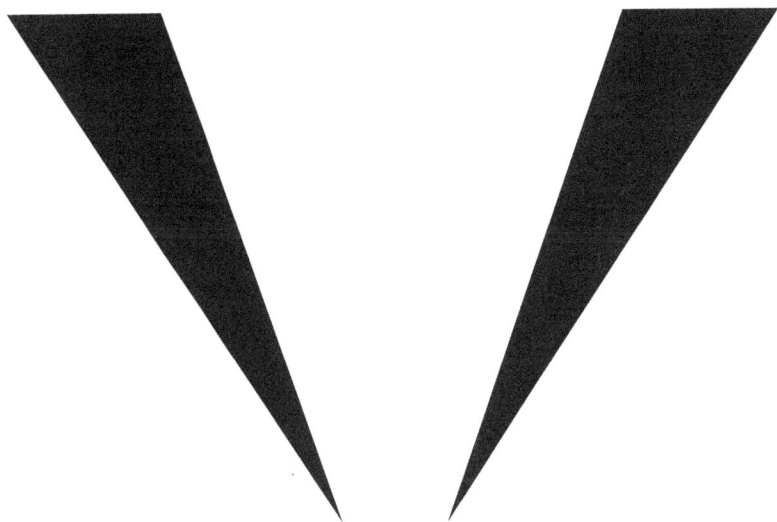

GOING HOLLYWOOD

a memoir by

Josh Becker

POINTBLANK

To Mom and Dad

"There are no shortcuts to anyplace worth going"
—*Beverly Sills*

Part I:

Going Hollywood

July, 1976.

L.A. was a smoggy white-hot furnace as I got off the 10 at Arlington, then drove north through a bleak section of town into Hollywood. I had to keep squinting my eyes to see through the overexposed glare. "Okay, everything needs to be two stops darker," I mumbled to myself. Arlington Avenue veered to the left, then mysteriously became Wilton Place, which then split off with Van Ness Avenue As I took the Van Ness fork, I thought, "I've *got* to rent an apartment today, 'cause I absolutely can't stay where I'm staying anymore."

Where I was staying was an apartment that belonged to a friend of a friend of my dad, that had once belonged to the guy's mother, but she died a few years earlier. For some insane reason the guy had just kept the apartment, although he never went there, nor had he even cleaned it since the old lady expired. The place was incredibly creepy, stunk of mothballs and death, and was located in Rancho Park, a scary, completely Mexican neighborhood in south L.A. I'd already been there for a few days with my buddy Stan, from Detroit, who drove out to L.A. with me, and that was okay. But Stan had left the day before yesterday, and there was just no way I could handle going back to that place for another night. There was a life-sized bust of Julius Caesar in the master bedroom silhouetted against a window that scared the shit out of me every time I walked past. Stan and I had both slept on the floor in the living room in our sleeping bags.

Approaching Melrose Boulevard, I spotted the "Apt for Rent" sign on the front of a faded yellow apartment building marked 666 North Van Ness. I pulled my yellow Mazda rotary wagon over to the right and stopped. I glanced to my left, then did a double-take.

Kitty-cornered from where I presently sat was Paramount Pictures Studios. The movie studio lot was surrounded by an 8-foot tall, 2-foot thick, tan stucco wall. It looked like a fortress, with guards at the gate and everything.

"*Holy shit!*" I proclaimed. "*It's Paramount Pictures!*"

It's not like I'd never seen Paramount Pictures before—I had (from the outside). But I hadn't put it together when I was getting directions to this building that Paramount was on *this* corner. So I'd be living directly across the street, if I took the apartment, that is.

"It's an omen," I said aloud.

Having spent my entire youth going to every movie I possibly could, as well as having sneaked and stayed up most every night to watch *The Late Show*, then often *The Late Late Show*, too, I actually knew quite a bit about movies for someone a month shy of 18 years old. I knew, for example, that Paramount was where Billy Wilder had made a lot of his movies, like *Double Indemnity* and *Sunset Blvd.* Among many, many others, Paramount had also produced most of Preston Sturges's films, like *Sullivan's Travels* and *The Palm Beach Story*, and of course they had also produced the much more recent films, *The Godfather* and *The Godfather Part II*, two of my all-time favorite movies.

As I sat there in my car smoking a cigarette, gazing at the southwest corner of Paramount studios, with black and white images of Barbara Stanwyck and Fred MacMurray floating through my head, I thought, "I'm going to be a movie writer-director someday, just like Billy Wilder or Francis Coppola, and I'm going to make movies right *there*."

A knock on the passenger window startled me back to reality. Standing at the window was a middle-aged man with a reddish-blond mustache, no shirt, tight designer jeans, and a cowboy hat and boots. A big beer gut hung over his belt. He pointed and said, "Josh?"

I nodded, got out of the car, went around and shook the man's hand. "Dan?"

"Yeah. You lookin' for an apartment?" he asked with a slight southern drawl.

I nodded, "That's me."

"Okay, come on."

Dan started toward the building just as a highly effeminate Mexican boy came flouncing down the stairs trailing a pungent cloud of cologne.

Dan shook his head. "Fuckin' faggots," he snorted, spitting on the sidewalk for punctuation. "The building's full of 'em. Black ones, white ones, big ones, little ones, old ones, young ones, you name it." Dan looked me up and down suspiciously—I was 5-foot-10, 165, with short brown hair, and a full dark beard.

Dan asked, "How old are you?"

I said, "I'm 21."

Dan seemed momentarily skeptical, then shrugged, turned and clomped his pointy cowboy boots up the red concrete steps leading to the front door of the building. I internally sighed. That was a close one. But what if he makes me prove I'm 21? Then I'm screwed.

Meanwhile, the faded yellow three-story stucco apartment building didn't look *too* bad from outside. Being located just off Melrose Boulevard, a central artery in L.A., was convenient, and of course it was right across from Paramount Pictures, so it had that going for it, too. Still, as I looked around, it sure seemed like kind of a crappy neighborhood, with the unmistakable vibe of a slum. In the center of the big parking lot directly across the street, an old black wino sat teetering on a milk crate while drinking something from a bottle inside a brown paper bag.

I turned around and saw the address above the door just as Dan walked under it. I said, "Six-six-six."

Dan nodded. "Yeah. Like that devil kid in the movie."

I thought, *The Omen*, but I didn't say anything. The less chatter the better. Then I thought, "Hey, didn't I just say 'omen' a minute ago? Hmmm?"

Dan entered the dark foyer with me following along behind. It was dim even in the daytime with the lights on. The floor was covered with worn red carpeting that smelled musty and old. On one wall of the foyer was a big mural of a black Jesus, his cloaked arms outstretched toward a multitude of children and animals, almost shockingly amateurish in its execution. Dan turned right and went up the stairs with me tagging along after him.

"So, what brings you to L.A., Josh? Where'd you say you were from?"

"Michigan. Um, I'm going to film school. I'm gonna be a movie director, and writer."

Dan nodded, "Really? Where you goin'? UCLA?"

I sighed and shook my head, "No."

"USC?"

"Uh, no. I'm going to Columbia College. Over on La Brea."

"Oh, yeah. Across from the Bargain Circus, right?"

I nodded sadly, "Right." People didn't say, "Oh, that's where Francis Ford Coppola went to school," or "That's where George Lucas went to school," but "Oh, yeah, that's across from the Bargain Circus, right?" That's how people in L.A. seemed to know Columbia College—by its convenient location near a particularly cheap store. But Columbia's ad in the back of *Super 8 Filmaker Magazine* had looked pretty impressive to me, with the word "Accredited" in boldface that seemed to have some meaning to my mom and dad.

On the second floor, Dan stepped up to the door marked 7, unlocked it, and opened the door. Inside was a barren, clean, studio apartment with a folded-up Murphy bed in the wall, a small kitchen, and a small bathroom. Dan pulled down the squeaky Murphy bed.

"A hundred and twenty-five dollars a month."

I'd already looked at enough apartments to be unimpressed. I shrugged, "A hundred and twenty-five dollars a month and no bedroom?"

"Well, yeah. But it's a good deal. It's clean."

I waved my hand, turning to leave. "I'll think about it."

"Wait," said Dan. "I know *just* what you're looking for."

He closed the door to number 7, turned, took three steps over to the first door off the second floor landing marked number 6, and opened the door. This apartment was tiny, literally the size of a bedroom, 12-by-12, with no kitchen, a very small bathroom, a hotplate, and a dorm room-sized fridge. Presently, it was also jammed to the ceiling with old furniture.

Dan said, "Sixty-five dollars a month, including utilities. Now, come on, you can't beat that."

Without any hesitation I said, "I'll take it."

Dan said, "Great. It's yours. Gimme a hand, we'll get some of this shit outta here."

Dan and I began hauling furniture out of the miniature apartment. I thought, "That's it? I've got my own apartment in Hollywood. Fucking-A! It all begins, the true history of Hollywood, which of course must include me."

A tall, square-jawed, middle-aged man with greasy, jet black hair came down the stairs wearing a black and white Japanese kimono. His strong cologne actually preceded him. Just the way he held the robe together with his other hand limp-wristedly dangling free, I knew he was gay. Very gay.

Dan said, "Josh, this is the manager, Rex. Rex, this is Josh. What's the last name?"

I said, "Becker."

Rex held out his redolent, limp-wristed hand, as though he expected it to be kissed, and stated, "Rex Roberts."

As I shook Rex's hand, I now knew that my own hand stank of his pungent cologne, too, but I resisted the urge to wipe it off so as to not be impolite.

Dan said, "Josh's gonna be a film director. Rex is an actor." Dan looked at me like he'd just gotten a brilliant idea. "Hey! You can put Rex in one of your movies."

Rex's eyes lit up. "You're going to be a film director, are you?"

I nodded, "Well, yeah. I mean, that's why I'm out here in California."

Rex turned and headed quickly back up the stairs, holding his kimono closed. "I'll be right back."

Dan and I watched Rex mince his way up the stairs. We exchanged a look that said, "My God is that guy gay."

Dan and I finished clearing out the apartment. Of the large selection of crappy old furniture, I chose a single bed; a small wooden desk painted white with thick house paint so that the drawers wouldn't close properly; a matching white wooden chair; one-third of a worn, greenish, sectional couch; two ugly lamps; and a day-glo orange easy chair that appeared like it might be comfortable, until you sat down on it, that is—then you found out very abruptly that it actually had no cushion at all and was solid particle board—it was a prop easy chair. The apartment was now completely furnished.

Rex reappeared and handed me an 8-by-10 photo. "Here's my headshot. When you get settled in we'll have to have a glass of wine and talk movies. I've been in a few, you know."

I said, "Yeah. Sure. That'd be great."

Rex went back up the stairs.

Dan said, "So, first, last, and security deposit comes to $195." He held out his hand.

I took out my wallet and counted out $200 in twenties. Dan struggled to get his hand into his ridiculously tight blue jeans pocket, pulled out a huge wad of cash, peeled off a five, and handed it to me.

"There ya go. Welcome to the neighborhood."

Dan casually reached down and gave my ass a squeeze, then turned and clomped down the steps. I stood there with the five-dollar bill in my hand, feeling utterly confused, thinking, "But didn't he just say, 'Faggots, old ones, young ones, green ones, blue ones . . .'? Huh."

I put the money in my pocket, then glanced down at the headshot in my hand. On one side was a close-up of Rex Roberts looking dapper and handsome, in a greasy kind of way; on the other side was a composite of smaller photos of Rex in various outfits: in one he was wearing a hardhat and work boots, pointing at something with a totally limp wrist; in another shot he was wearing a tuxedo and holding a futuristic-looking pistol, but once again with his wrist preposterously limp. I shook my head, "Oh, man, what kind of nuthouse am I moving into?" Tossing the headshot into the apartment, I went downstairs to get my stuff out of the car.

I brought in my boxes, my records, and my Radio Shack stereo, which I immediately set up. I thought seriously about what the first record I played in my new pad should be, then put on David Bowie's "Diamond Dogs."

I then immediately went about coating all of the walls with movie posters: *A Clockwork Orange, Lolita, The Exorcist,* and *The Harder They Fall,* as well as many black and white 8-by-10 movie stills of James Cagney about to punch one of the Dead End Kids in *Angels With Dirty Faces*; Humphrey Bogart, Mary Astor, Sydney Greenstreet, and Peter Lorre all looking down at *The Maltese Falcon*; and Ray Milland reaching for a drink in *The Lost Weekend.*

I then set up my Smith-Corona electric typewriter on the desk, plugged it in, turned it on, and listened to its loud motor whir. The motor was so loud and uneven that if I left it running for any length of time the typewriter would crawl across the desk, in a feeble attempt to escape my abuse. I inserted a piece of white typing paper in the carriage, poised my fingers over the keys, then glanced up.

Peering out the window across Van Ness Avenue, there was the parking lot with the drunk old black man sitting on milk crate at the center. Across from that was Producer's Studio, a much smaller film studio than Paramount, located directly across Melrose. On the bricks on the side of one of the soundstages of Producer's Studio, I could still make out the name "Clune," in old, knobby-looking lettering, that I immediately assumed must be the film studio's original name back in the early days of silent pictures.

"Oh, cool!"

Between the old soundstage and Melrose was a 1940s strip mall with a liquor store, a revival movie house called the Encore Theater, and an old Jerry's Market. Across Melrose was the Hollywood Executive Apartments, a shit-hole of a building, with Club Tentacion on the ground floor blaring loud salsa music out the open door.

To my left, on the south side of the sprawling parking lot, was Walter Allen Studio Plant Rental, where a jungle of potted plants waited to be rented to any local production needing greenery. Next door to that was Castex Prop Rentals, carrying everything from stuffed tigers to Roman columns.

With my fingers still poised over the typewriter's keys, I mumbled, "I can't think of anything to write." I lit a cigarette, looked around the little apartment, then sighed deeply. I stood up, crossed the living room in two steps, shut the door, and locked it.

I sat down on the one-third of a couch. I took a small bag of marijuana and pack of Zig-Zag papers from my pocket. I deftly rolled a slim joint, lit up, took a big hit, then held it in for a second. I slowly blew out a thick cloud of pot smoke into the bright L.A. sunlight streaming in almost horizontally through my west-facing windows.

I said, "Wow! My own pad. In Hollywood."

Opening my wallet, I looked at the photo of my girlfriend, Renée. Her pose in the picture clearly said, "Oh, shit! Don't take my picture!" Renée was a pretty, curvy, well-built blonde, and I was stuck on her bad. I rolled my eyes and spoke disdainfully, "*My girlfriend*. She has to go and *finally* get serious on me the week I leave?"

I thought about the night two weeks ago, right before I left for L.A. Renée finally put out, after weeks of daily courting, and hours of smooching in her dad's den. We did it on the couch in her parents' house after everyone else had gone to sleep.

Renée had been my girlfriend five years earlier at summer camp, when we were both 13. We spent a lot of time that summer kissing and touching, but never going any further. It was a truly wonderful, fun, sexy summer romance that lasted a few weeks after camp, then ended because we went to different junior high schools.

On the first day of the 1975 fall semester at Eastern Michigan University in Ypsilanti, Michigan, I was walking up the hill from the dorm to the classroom buildings. I found myself walking behind a curvy blonde girl in a green and white striped dress, with a terrific ass and beautiful shapely legs. I nodded appreciatively, thinking to myself, "Now that's my idea of a great ass. Nice legs, too."

I sped up to see if the face was as good as the body. As I passed her and looked back I saw that it was Renée. I couldn't believe it, and neither could Renée. Our meeting seemed highly fortuitous.

Renée and I went and had coffee at the student union. I asked, "What are you doing in college? Shouldn't you be in 12th grade?"

Renée said, "I could ask you the same thing, right?"

I nodded. "Yeah, except this is my second year of college. I've already done two semesters at OCC."

"So, I graduated a year early, but you graduated two years early?"

I nodded again. "Yeah. I was always a precocious kid. I snuck in and took the GED test. Once I'd passed it and gotten a degree, how could my parents possibly make me go back to high school?"

Renée smiled. "Impressive." She then told me the heartbreaking tale of having just broken up with her boyfriend, Steve, who worked at a nearby men's wear store. I couldn't believe my luck. She was available, too.

I said, "Oh, that's too bad. I'm really sorry," and touched her hand.

Renée and I ended up back in my dorm room, quickly picking up where we'd left off five years earlier, at the kissing/touching stage. Over the next few days this rapidly progressed to the getting-naked stage, moving right along toward the sexual intercourse stage, which is exactly when her former boyfriend Steve called. It seemed that Steve was not her *former* boyfriend at all, but was in fact her *current* boyfriend. Steve, it turned out, was a big, handsome, well-built, blond fellow, with a hairy chest, always dressed in silk disco shirts unbuttoned to his belly button, who sadly had a pronounced lisp.

I answered the phone. "Hello?"

Steve said, *"Thith ith Th*teve. *Ith* Renée there?"

I put my hand over the receiver and imitated him, "It'*th Th*teve. *Ith* Renée here?"

Renée grabbed the phone out of my hands, "Hi, Steve. Oh, we were just watching TV and we fell asleep. I'll be back in a minute." She hung up the phone, leapt out of bed, and got dressed in a big hurry.

"I thought you and Steve had broken up?"

Renée said, "We pretty much have."

"Really? You're sure not acting like it."

She hastily got most of her clothes back on, gave me a kiss on the cheek, said, "I'll talk to you tomorrow," and split.

After several more weeks of Renée vacillating between Steve and me, causing me tremendous heartache and turmoil, I finally gave Renée the ultimatum.

"Look, it's either him or me!"

Renée thought about it for a few unendurable days, then said, "Him."

And thus ended the second chapter of Renée's and my romance.

As fate would have it, at some point during the next semester, the men's wear store where Steve worked had a party at a hotel on the third floor. Steve and two other salesmen were out on the balcony leaning back against the railing facing in when the rail gave way. Steve fell first, then the two other guys landed on top of him, apparently breaking every bone in his body.

Soon thereafter I got accepted to the University of Michigan, and so, after just the one term at EMU, I quit, packed up my shit, and moved the five miles from Ypsilanti to Ann Arbor.

After one frozen winter semester at U of M, where my previous grade point of 4.0 plummeted to a 1.9, I decided, "That's it, I'm moving to Hollywood." In the interim, however, I temporarily moved back into my parents' house in the suburbs of Detroit.

That's when Renée called.

And so we hooked back up yet again, even though I'd already made my plans to move to L.A. Every day for a couple of weeks I went over to Renée's parents' house, where Renée was living for the summer, and we would kiss and hold hands and make out and even touch everywhere, but never go all the way. Renée was tormenting me, saying shit like, "Why are you moving to L.A.?" while she squeezed my aching woody through my jeans.

"'Cause that's where the film business is," I gulped.

She took my hand and put it directly on her warm crotch, rubbing it against the slightly moist fabric of her pants. "But *I'm* here."

So, the night before I left for L.A., sitting on the couch in her parents' living room with the lights out, we kissed and touched, and at the point where she'd always previously stopped me, she now *didn't* stop me. Before I knew it I had Renée's pants unzipped and my hand inside her panties. In a few moments we both had our pants down. Then Renée and I went at it like wild animals in heat for a few minutes.

When I was about to come, I said, "I'm about to come."

Renée said, "Pull out," which I did. Then she said, "But don't come on the couch." So I leaned back and shot off all over my shirt, and it was totally overwhelming. It was such an intense relief after three weeks of constant foreplay that I burst out laughing. Renée looked at me in shock; she definitely didn't see the joke.

Renée whispered, "What are you laughing at?"

"I'm laughing because it felt so good."

"Are you laughing at me?"

"No."

Renée looked horrified, quickly pushed me off and pulled up her pants, then scrambled off the couch. "You're laughing because I finally let you go all the way and you're leaving tomorrow. What a stupid thing to do, right?"

I shook my head in bewilderment, whispering, "I'm telling you, I laughed because it felt so good."

Renée shook her head. "I don't believe you. You're laughing at me."

"I am not."

"What the hell are we doing? Look, just go to Hollywood already, okay?" She walked out of the living room, went straight up the steps, turned the corner and disappeared out of sight.

I pulled up my own pants, shaking my head in confusion. I looked down at my fucked up shirt.

"Oh, man, it was all going so well, what happened?"

I called Renée the next day from the road and she would barely speak to me, basically giving me the brush-off. Well, I was moving out of town, but still . . .

But still, I had it for her bad. Real bad.

I took a big hit on my little joint, sucking a third of it down in one puff and making myself cough. Smoke and spittle spiraled through the last rays of warm setting sunlight beaming in through the windows of my apartment. In Hollywood. Across from Paramount, for Christ's sake.

And yet, as I sat there in the growing dark in this tiny little apartment, I suddenly felt extremely alone. All by myself in an alien place. The little roach between my fingertips had gone out and was now too small to relight.

I walked over to one of the ugly lamps and turned the switch. Click, nothing. I checked and it was plugged in, so that meant the bulb was blown. I tried the other lamp and its bulb was dead, too. I flicked the wall switch and the exposed overhead light didn't work, either. Sighing, I dropped into the orange chair with a *thunk!* as my tailbone hit the solid particle board.

"*Oww! Fuck!*"

I sat on the fake chair in the gathering gloom, all by myself. Not quite 18 years old, and 2,500 miles from home.

"Well," I said. "Here I am. Now what do I do?"

* * *

Directly across from my apartment, on the other side of a big empty parking lot, was the Encore Theater, a revival movie house. As it turned out the Encore was having a wonderful series of double-bills with the directors attending and doing Q&As between shows. I first saw Samuel Fuller between his films *Run of the Arrow* and *Verboten!* When someone asked why Rod Steiger never mentioned, nor even admitted to having made, Fuller's film *Run of the Arrow*, Sam Fuller removed his big cigar and replied gruffly, "That's because Steiger's an asshole." Sam Fuller then told us big

portions of the plot for his upcoming film, *The Big Red One*. I enjoyed the whole thing immensely, but as hard as I tried I couldn't think of a question for him. As I walked across the parking lot home after the movie, I felt ashamed that I hadn't had the knowledge or the wherewithal to come up with a single question.

Next in the series at the Encore was *The Last Picture Show*, which I'd already seen several times and was a film that I seriously loved. Also showing was the brand-new movie, *Nickelodeon*, with the director Peter Bogdanovich in attendance between the films. This time I spent all day formulating just the right question. That night at the screening I sat in the front row. After *The Last Picture Show*, Peter Bogdanovich came in wearing aviator shades and an ascot, and sat down in front of the audience. After a short oration, spoken a bit too quietly for such a large room with no PA system, he opened it up for questions. My hand shot right up. Bogdanovich turned to me and said, "Yes?"

I said, "Given how brilliant the black and white cinematography by the great Robert Surtees is in *The Last Picture Show*, why did you then switch and use László Kovács for black and white photography on *Paper Moon*, which is also gorgeous?"

Peter Bogdanovich looked at me with utter contempt and said, "I don't *use* a cinematographer, I *work* with him. Next?" And he took the next question.

I was mortified. My mouth hung open. I lowered myself back into my seat burning red-hot with humiliation mixed with indignation. It was a perfectly legitimate question, *goddamnit!* And I hadn't even gotten an answer, either.

At some point during the screening of the utterly miserable *Nickelodeon*, I thought to myself, "It's a good fucking thing you didn't come in *after* this piece of dogshit, you motherfucker!"

On my way out of the theater I passed the old man who apparently owned the place. He was about 75, wore a wrinkled, baggy, brown suit, with an unlit cigarette dangling from his lip. I had just put a cigarette in my mouth and was about to light it with my Zippo, but instead I reached out and offered the light to the old man.

"Here."

I lit the man's cigarette, then my own.

"Thank you," said the old man. "I've seen you here a lot lately."

I pointed over my shoulder with my thumb. "I moved into the building across the parking lot."

The old man nodded, "Oh, yeah, that shit-hole. You a movie fan, is that it?"

I nodded, "I sure am. I'm gonna be a director."

"Really? You ever run a projector?"

I shook my head. "Not a 35mm projector. I've run 16mm projectors."

The old man flicked his cigarette ash and shrugged. "Same fuckin' thing. You wanna job?"

I didn't hesitate. "Sure."

"Be here tomorrow at 5:00. I'll have the projectionist show you how to do it. It's easy." The old man tossed his cigarette into the street, then walked into the empty theater.

I couldn't believe my luck. I got to Hollywood and without even asking I was offered a job as a projectionist in a movie theater. How incredibly cool!

As I walked away from the theater I said, "Fuck Peter Bogdanovich and the horse he rode in on! How dare he make a movie I love like *The Last Picture Show. Asshole!*"

At 5:00 the next day I was already standing in front of the theater smoking a cigarette when the old man came walking up in what was very possibly the same baggy, wrinkled brown suit.

"You're prompt, that's good." He took out a pack of Winstons and put one in his mouth. I pulled out my Zippo and lit it for him. The old man looked at me, leaned forward, cupped his hands around mine, lit up and said, "Thanks."

In the old projection booth, covered with magazine pictures of naked women, I watched as a hairy-shouldered, middle-aged projectionist named Will, wearing a sleeveless undershirt, rewound a big reel of 35mm film on rewinds. He was working up quite a sweat and obviously didn't use deodorant, or bathe. The two projectors beside him were candidates for the Smithsonian—big, black, hulking, carbon-arc Simplex projectors from the 1940s, or maybe even the 1930s. Bits and pieces of copper-colored carbon rods, the width of a fat pencil, were literally everywhere.

"The trick," said Will, "is to keep the carbon rods as close together as possible to keep the flame as bright as possible. As the rods melt the flame goes down and the picture gets dim. Then you crank these knobs which causes the rods to move closer together. Get it?"

I nodded. "Sure."

"And since Lou's such a cheap son of a bitch, you have to keep making up new rods from the old ones with these little clips." Will held up a steel clip that allowed two halves of carbon rods to be affixed together into one whole one.

I looked around and among the eight million bits of carbon rods were three million of these clips.

Will showed me how to thread the projectors, which wasn't very hard. In fact, it was actually easier than threading a 16mm projector because the film is bigger. Will also showed me how to rewind the film back onto its original reel, then replace the reel in the octagonal metal Goldberg can. Big deal, a monkey could do that.

Will said, "You got it?"

I nodded, "I guess so."

"Good luck," and he left.

I stood in the old projection booth by myself and suddenly felt creepy as hell and horribly claustrophobic. I could feel my whole life flickering past in a time-lapse shot of me becoming a fat old smelly pervert projectionist like Will. A chill crept into the marrow of my bones. I could still smell Will's sweat permeating everything in the tiny cubicle and I suddenly felt nauseous. Since there was no smoking in the projection booth, I quickly dashed outside, took a big breath of air, then lit up.

JULY 31, 1976

I have decided that it definitely would be in my (and my typewriter's) best interest to write at least one thousand words a day. I don't really know whether I can keep it up, but I certainly hope so.

I think a good way to start each day, to kind of get things flowing, is to reinstate my journal. And so it was.

Today is the end of my first full month in California, and so far I have an apartment in Hollywood across from Paramount Pictures, and a job as a projectionist at a revival movie theater. Not bad.

Today I spent about five hours in the projection booth with Will who is teaching me the tricks of the projection trade. If he didn't stink so bad it would have been an enjoyable experience.

I have heard that very soon there will be an opening for a full-time projectionist at the Gordon Theater which is owned by the same guy who owns the Encore where I'm learning.

I've gotten only one letter since I have moved into 666 and that was from my sister Pam. I've written about 8 letters so I should be getting back bunches and bunches.

I really have to get some decent pot. The crap that I've been smoking is really shit.

Well, as best as I can figure it, one thousand words is about three and a half typed pages, double-spaced. Which reminds me, I'm going to submit another short story, "The Sins of Space," to a magazine, probably Galaxy. *I suppose I should try submitting "Expectations," but I can't think of what kind of magazine would take it.*

Now to the real writing.

Over the course of the next gruelingly long week, I projected unforgivably scratchy prints of the Moscow Ballet performing *Swan Lake* and *Sleeping Beauty*, both films twice each night. It was the most utterly stultifying, dull thing that I'd ever done in my life so far. I had a history teacher in high school who had previously held the position of The Most Boring Thing In the World, but now it was this job, hands down. Being a projectionist may have been a job in the movie business, but it was at entirely the wrong end of the movie business.

Every 20 minutes a bell would ring indicating that the reel had to be changed. This was the exciting part of the job, making the changeovers. I'd position myself between the two projectors, a wooden handle connected to each projector in both hand, peering out the little window at the movie watching for the changeover marks that appear every 20 minutes at the top right corner of the picture. If the second projector was properly loaded, when I saw the second changeover mark, usually a circle, although sometimes a star, I would pull the left handle while simultaneously pushing the right one. The left projector would shut down just as the right projector came on and the film would flow seamlessly into the next reel. If you did it right, that is.

I would then take the reel of film off the stopped projector, rewind it, and put it back in its can. Then I'd load that projector up with the next reel.

Ding, ding, ding.

Changeover.

Rewind.

Reload.

Ding, ding, ding . . .

I stepped out of the theater after Saturday night's showings. Four hours of my life shot down the toilet, never to be gotten back. I lit a cigarette and shook my bleary head. "Maybe," I mumbled to myself, "it wouldn't be so bad if they were movies I liked. But fucking ballet movies, *Jesus fucking Christ!*"

Lou, the old owner, stepped up.

"You're doing a good job."

"Thanks."

"It's not so hard, is it?"

"No, not really."

"You wanna drink?"

I shrugged. "Okay."

"I live right around the block," said Lou. "Come on."

Lou and I walked around the block to a spooky, old, dark brick apartment building. Lou's apartment was huge, though dusty and unkempt, and it smelled like mothballs and urine. Lou filled two glasses with bourbon and water on the rocks and handed me one. I hated bourbon, but I took a sip anyway, smiling, thinking, "*Yuk!*"

Lou sat down in an easy chair and I sat on a lumpy brown leather couch. Lou took a big drink and lit a cigarette. I also lit a cigarette. Neither of us spoke. Lou finally said . . .

"So, you wanna suck my cock?"

I said, "No."

"You sure?"

"Yeah, I'm sure."

"Want me to suck your cock?"

"No, not really."

"You want that job?"

"Not enough to suck your cock, or have you suck mine."

"Then it was nice knowing you. You're now officially unemployed."

I set down the horrid drink and stood up. I said, "You owe me for the week."

"Yeah? How about you come by tomorrow and I'll give you check."

I stepped forward so that I was looming over the little old man. "How about you just give it to me right now. Twenty-five bucks a night times six nights. One hundred and fifty bucks." I held my hand out in Lou's face.

"Don't get excited," said Lou reaching into his pocket. He pulled out a wad of cash, counted out the bills and handed them to me. "Here."

I took the money, counted it, then turned to leave.

Lou said, "You sure you don't wanna suck my cock? I'll give you another hundred bucks."

"I'm positive," I said and left.

Outside in the fresh cool night air I took a deep breath. Was everybody some kind of fucking freak in this town? I flicked my cigarette and started to walk home.

"Oh, great. Now I've gotta find another job."

* * * *

While I was unemployed I began going to the movies every single day, sometimes twice a day. This was something that was simply not possible back in Detroit, and one of the reasons I'd wanted to move to L.A. in the first place (among others)—the sheer volume of movies showing all the time. I went to every movie theater up and down Hollywood Boulevard, from the ritzy Mann's Chinese (formerly Grauman's) at the western end of the boulevard (which actually goes on for a few more blocks, but then becomes residential and dead-ends into a park), all the way down to the eastern end of Hollywood Boulevard, meaning Western Avenue (Hollywood Boulevard continues east for several miles past Western, but no one really walks there), to the World Theater where they showed second-run triple-bills for 99 cents and every seat in the house was broken. It made absolutely no difference to me if the films looked like they might be any good, or if they got positive reviews—I pretty much just saw everything that was playing everywhere.

Eventually, however, no matter what I did, I always had to return to my tiny little apartment and face up to being alone yet another night, with absolutely no friends to see or call. I was discovering the real meaning of deep, lengthy solitude, and it was driving me slightly insane.

One night, feeling particularly lonely, I went to see an Akira Kurosawa double-bill of *Hidden Fortress* and *Those Who Tread on Tiger's Tails* at the Fairfax Theater on Beverly and Fairfax. In the lobby between the films I saw a tall blond fellow standing alone smoking. I lit my own cigarette, casually stepped up to the guy and, trying not to come off as gay, asked, "So, what did you think of the film?"

The blond guy shrugged and winced. "I don't like these kinds of movies. Do you?"

"Yeah, I do. Then what are you doing here?"

"My friends convinced me that I should see it."

I puffed on my cig. "Oh. Are you staying for the next film?"

"No."

"Oh."

We both smoked for a second. Finally the guy asked . . .

"Are you a big movie fan, or are you gay and trying to pick me up?"

I quickly said, "Movie fan."

"Well, I'm not."

My smile faded. "Gay or a movie fan?"

"Neither." The guy took out a business card and a pen. "If you're *really* a movie fan, you'll like these friends of mine. The ones that talked me into seeing this. There's this whole house full of movie nuts." He wrote down a list of first names and a phone number, then handed me the card. "Really, you'll like these guys. They live about a mile from here on Sixth Street."

I took the card. "Thanks."

"No problem." The blond guy stubbed out his smoke, then turned and walked out of the theater.

I looked down at what was written on the back of the business card. It said:

James
Brad
Bill
Larry
Inigo
Sherman
(213) 555-1212

I looked up from the card a week later. As usual, I was alone at night in my tiny apartment. I was watching *Mary Hartman, Mary Hartman* on my little orange plastic black and white TV set. "Oh, what the hell," I thought, picking up the receiver of the phone and spinning the rotary dial with my finger. The phone rang twice, then was answered by a male voice.

"Hello?"

I looked down at the card and got nervous. "Uh, is this James?"

"No."

"Brad?"

"No."

"Bill?"

"No."

"Larry?"

"No."

"Inigo?"

"No."

"Sherman?"

"Speaking."

I explained how I'd gotten the number.

Sherman said, "Yeah, that's Peter. He's a carpenter. He doesn't like foreign movies. I can't believe he went and saw *Hidden Fortress*."

I said, "He didn't like it."

"I'm not surprised. Did you?"

"Yeah, I did. I hear it's the basis for George Lucas's new sci-fi movie that he's shooting right now."

"Yeah," said Sherman, "that's what we were telling Peter. I'm sure that's why he went and saw it."

Sherman explained that he was attending the American Film Institute in Beverly Hills with the intention of becoming a filmmaker, either a director or a cinematographer, he wasn't quite sure yet. I said that I intended to be a director, as well as a writer, and that I would be going to Columbia College next semester. Sherman burst out laughing.

"What?"

"I went there last semester," said Sherman. "It's a waste of time."

"Really? I kind of suspected as much."

"Yeah. It's for the future grips and production assistants of the world."

Sherman and I talked casually about movies for an hour, then we hung up. I thought, "That's the coolest guy I've talked to since getting here. He knows his shit."

A week later I called again. This time when I heard Sherman's voice I said, "Sherman?"

"Speaking."

We yakked for another hour and it was great—the best movie conversation I'd had since I'd gotten out there. I really liked talking with this guy. Although, by the end of the conversation we still had made no plans to get together, and there were no invitations. I shrugged as I hung up.

"Huh. It's not so easy making friends with people out here."

* * * *

Just as Sherman had predicted, Columbia College quickly turned out to be a total waste of time. Worse still, nobody was even friendly, nor did any of them actually seem interested in movies. And even worse than that, there wasn't one cute girl in the whole school. Another thing I didn't like about Columbia College was that all of the classes were held in the evening, a time I *never* felt like going to school.

I had a TV direction class that could have been interesting had it not been taught by a bombastic, 300-pound, loud-mouth asshole who thought he was Orson Welles and seemed to derive great pleasure from yelling at all the students. A TV director has to call for actions in a precise manner. Specifically, they must give everyone a warning before they cue them, such as, "Ready on camera one," "Take camera one," "Ready on the announcer," "Cue the announcer," etc. The rule in the class was that if you didn't ask for something properly, it wasn't done. Unfortunately, many of the students had recently arrived from foreign lands, particularly Japan and Korea, and quite a few didn't speak much, or any, English. A Japanese boy said, "Ah, take-a the announcer," and the fat asshole teacher went nuts.

"Take the announcer *where*? You have to *cue* the announcer. Get the fuck out of the director's chair!"

I had no problem speaking the directions properly, but I still got yelled at for cutting too quickly. No matter what you did, you were going to get hollered at.

In another class, we spent an hour and a half coiling and uncoiling electrical cables. The idea was that if you coiled the cable properly, you could then hold onto one end and just throw it and it would uncoil without knotting. This was certainly practical information, if not exactly what I was envisioning when I dreamed of moving to Hollywood and going to film school.

It only took a few weeks before I wanted to quit. Columbia College was every bit as big a waste of time as Sherman had said it was. But if I quit before the end of the semester I knew I'd really get serious shit from my parents, so I just grit my teeth and stuck it out.

One night I stayed late after classes were over to use the school's Super 8 editing equipment. I'd brought with me four 50-foot reels of sound Super 8 footage that I'd shot back in Michigan right before I left. These were the dailies of a short movie entitled *The Case of the Topanga Pearl*, a comedy detective story, starring myself as the detective, and some neighborhood/school acquaintances, Sam Raimi, Scott Spiegel and Ellen Sandweiss. We shot the entire movie in one day at my parents' house, and it was a lot of fun.

My best buddy for years was Ivan Raimi, Sam's older brother, and the Raimis lived around the block from me. One day as I was walking around Franklin, I ran into Sam, who was a year younger than me, and he said, "Me and some guys from school, Bruce Campbell and Scott Spiegel, have been making movies lately. I know you love movies. Would you like to see our newest film?"

I said, "Sure."

Sam had usurped the back bedroom at his parents' house as his studio/editing suite. He showed me the 12-minute, sound Super 8 film *Six Months to Live* on the wall. It was entirely slapstick comedy gags vaguely tied together with a plot about a guy who's been told he has six months to live. I laughed all the way through it, not to mention I admired some of Sam's filmmaking techniques. It was a good film, better than anything I'd made yet.

"Wow," I said. "That was really good."

"Thanks," said Sam.

"We should make a movie together."

"Sure. Write a script."

I did just that. I called it *The Case of the Topanga Pearl*, and right before I left for L.A. we shot it all in one day, and it was a complete gas. We all had a terrific time, and Sam gave a very funny performance as the Peter Lorre-like little German weasel character that he played entirely on his knees. The best bit of dialogue was when Sam sticks a pistol into the femme fatale's face. She says, "You wouldn't kill me, Fritz. You loved me once." He says (with a German accent), "Be thankful. Now I will only kill you once!"

So I watched each of the four three-minute reels of films. There were some funny bits, and couple of cool angles—like when the detective, played by me, is drunk with his head on the desk, there's a sideways POV of each of the characters entering—but it didn't seem like there was enough footage to make it all cut together. Also, in the middle of the one take of Scott's zany prologue as an old man—wearing a very false beard made of cotton balls—that explained the entire upcoming plot, the film began to flash, then rolled out.

I sighed. I had the whole film cut together in a few hours, then I watched it all the way through. It ended up being about five minutes long, and it made a fair amount of sense, but just not enough sense, not as far as I was concerned. It was missing coverage, like a long shot of the house where it all took place, for example. And I really needed that first prologue shot of Scott, which I couldn't reshoot because I was here in L.A. and Scott was back in Michigan. *Shit!*

All in all, the film was a disappointment. But it was fun to make, and totally easy to set up. Sam, Scott, and Ellen couldn't have been nicer or more enjoyable to work with. And Sam got a few laughs entirely through his performance that had nothing to do with the script. Still, it wasn't a good movie. Interesting, but somewhat inept.

It was past midnight when I cleaned up the editing room, took my little reels of Super 8 film and went home.

* * * *

One day I found a film crew set up in front of the Encore Theater.

I asked one of the crew people, "What are you shooting?"

The crew guy said, "It's a TV show called *Future Cop*."

I nodded, "Huh." I'd never heard of it.

As I walked past a row of parked police cars, there was Ernest Borgnine all by himself in a policeman's uniform drinking a cup of coffee while sitting on the hood of a police car.

I immediately got a strange electrical sensation from seeing someone famous. So far I hadn't seen any other famous people. As I walked by, I offhandedly asked, "So, what'd ya wanna do tonight, Marty?"

Ernest Borgnine instantly displayed his warm, gap-toothed smile and replied, "I don't know, what do *you* want to do?"

Another day I walked into the Jerry's Market across the street from my apartment building and found a film crew shooting a Charmin toilet tissue commercial. Turning the corner, I literally ran into the actor (Dick Wilson) who played Mr. Whipple.

"Excuse me," I said.

"No problem," said Mr. Whipple. "Excuse me."

I couldn't help myself and said, "*Please*, don't squeeze the Charmin."

Mr. Whipple nodded, "You said it, brother."

Late one night as I was going out to my car to drive up to the Winchell's Donuts on Western Avenue, an old man stepped up to a stunning, two-tone, black and gray 1959 Studebaker Hawk parked behind my car.

I said to the old man, "1959 Hawk?"

The old man nodded, "Yes, indeed. Very good. How'd you know?"

"I'm from Detroit. It's beautiful. Did you buy it new?"

"Sure did. I went to buy a Mercedes-Benz, and Studebakers were sold at the same dealerships back then. I test-drove a diesel Mercedes first and it was so goddamn gutless it wouldn't pull a sick whore off a piss-pot. So then I test drove the Studebaker, and

I bought it. And I've driven it ever since. Helluva good car."

The old man and I both lit cigarettes.

I asked, "If you don't mind me asking, what are you doing up so late?"

The old man said, "I'm a locksmith at Paramount Pictures. I've been working there since 1930. Forty-six years now. I've changed locks for everybody: Marlene Dietrich, Gary Cooper, Maurice Chevalier, Jeanette McDonald—you name 'em, I changed their locks. They was always lockin' themselves outta their dressing rooms, or they'd be losin' their keys. Many a time I changed the locks for both Adolph Zukor and Jesse Lasky, two of the original pioneers of movies who started Paramount back in 1913. Jesse Lasky was a real gentleman. Zukor was a mean old son of a bitch."

"Adolph Zukor just died," I said. "He was a hundred and three."

The old locksmith nodded, puffing on his cigarette, "Oh, yeah. And Jesse Lasky died 20 years ago, not all that old, in hock up to his ears to the IRS, a broken man." He shrugged helplessly. "But, hell, what are you gonna do? Nobody ever said life was fair, right?"

I shrugged. Wasn't it? The old locksmith dropped his cigarette butt on the ground and squashed it out. Then, just as he must have done a hundred thousand times before since 1930, he took a heavy canvas tool bag out of the back seat of his car, made sure the doors were locked, then slowly made his way a block up Van Ness to Lemon Grove Avenue, which is the side employee entrance to Paramount.

I purchased a new typewriter ribbon and package of typing paper at Bargain Circus for 99 cents each, and was now attempting to use both of them. Strangely, the paper was inordinately thick, almost cardboard, while the ink in the ribbon was too thick and sticky and kept smearing, annoying the living shit out me.

I typed . . .

> Dear Renee:
> I deeply miss you. I think about you all the time. More than I should I'm sure. More than you probably think about me. But I can't help it, I love you.
> I'm really sorry we haven't been able to talk on the

phone, but I can't afford the long distance. And every time I call, you're not there anyway. I've spoken to your mom six times.

I've been thinking a lot about it, and I really think you should move out here and live with me. It's a small place, but we could find a bigger one. And we'd be together. Here in Hollywood. Wouldn't that be cool?

Think about it, okay?

I love you.

Honestly,

Josh

I folded up the thick paper and stuck it into an envelope. I stuck a stamp on it and put it on top of the mailbox for the postman to take away, which he did the next day.

And a week went by, then another, then another. Every time I passed the mailbox I'd check, most times knowing that no new mail had been delivered since the last time I'd checked.

The manager of 666 North Van Ness, Rex Roberts, an occasional actor and extra, told me that he was pretty visible at the end of *Whatever Happened to Baby Jane?* as one of the young people dancing around Joan Crawford on the beach. Rex had a variety of young male lovers who stayed with him a week or two, then moved on. Rex's present lover was named Johnny, a short, cute, Mexican boy with long eyelashes, who stuck around for several months. Rex had introduced Johnny and me on the stairs at some point previously.

One night there was a knock at my door. I answered it and found Johnny standing there, looking demure, batting his long eyelashes.

"Mind if I come in?" he purred.

I wasn't 100 percent sure what that meant, but since I was lonely, I said, "Sure. Come on in. You're Johnny, right?"

"Yeah, and you're Josh, right?"

"Right."

We shook hands and I was surprised to find that Johnny had quite a firm, manly handshake for a cute little gay Mexican boy imitating Marilyn Monroe.

Johnny stepped into the center of the small room and turned around. "Rex said you were looking for some pot."

I nodded eagerly. "Yeah. I am. You know where I can get some?"

"Sure," said Johnny, taking a bag from the pocket of his tight jeans. "Here, roll one up."

I smiled, took the bag and said, "Sure thing. Sit down. Would you like some coffee, milk, or water? That's all I've got."

"I'll take some coffee, thanks." Johnny sat down on the bed.

I put the kettle on the hotplate and turned it up to high. I asked, "Milk? Sugar?"

"Both. So, you don't have a kitchen, huh?"

"Nope, just a hotplate."

I sat down on the couch and rolled a joint. Since Johnny didn't seem to care, nor was he paying the slightest bit of attention, I rolled a big fatty, letting a lot of excess pot drop out the ends of the joint into my fruitcake tin. It seemed like pretty good shit, too. I toasted up the joint, and Johnny and I smoked it. Soon, we were stoned and laughing like old friends. Johnny pointed at the movie posters and stills.

"You're a big movie fan, huh?"

I nodded. "Yeah. I'm gonna be a film director, and a screen-writer."

Johnny nodded, then confided in me. "You know, I'm an artist, too."

"Oh, really?" I said, very interested. "What do you do?"

Johnny proudly replied, "I create relationships."

"What do you mean?" I asked, confused.

"I create relationships. Where there wasn't a relationship, I create one."

"How?" I asked, attaching a roach-clip to the joint.

"Well," said Johnny, "I look around the bar until I spot some-one I like, then I just stare at him."

"You don't go pick 'em up?"

Johnny shook his head in disgust. "No. Never. I just look at him. And when he finally looks back, I've caught him. Then I lure him over. It always works."

I looked at him intently to make sure he wasn't joking. He wasn't. He meant it.

I asked, "So, can you get me some more of this pot?"

"Sure. Gimme 10 bucks and you can have the rest of that."

Okay," I said, giving Johnny 10 bucks. There was about a quarter of an ounce here. "Thanks a lot."

"No problem. And when I get some more I'll stop by, okay?"

"Terrific. Please do."

"Okay. I'll see you later."

Johnny stepped up to the door, turned back, and batted his long eyelashes. "Nice meeting you."

"You, too."

Johnny left.

I relit the big fat roach, took a hit and shook my head.

"Ah, Hollywood."

Johnny and I became pothead acquaintances. Anytime Johnny had some weed he'd drop by and share it with me. I would tell Johnny about movies, and Johnny would tell me about his "artistic creations," meaning picking up guys in gay bars.

Johnny never propositioned me, nor made the slightest sexual overture. Even though I wouldn't have accepted anyway, after a few of Johnny's visits, I found to my surprise that I was slightly offended.

I sat there finishing the fat roach Johnny left behind, muttering to myself, "What's the matter? Aren't I attractive enough for him? Or maybe he just likes older guys, that must be it. And why do I care?"

I signed up at the Job Factory on Westwood Boulevard, right next door to the cool record store, Rhino Records. Every day I'd drive to Westwood and get a freshly updated list of crappy job openings. Oddly, there were never any jobs in the movie industry on the list.

> *AUGUST 3, 1976*
> *Started work today and boy oh boy was it lousy. It really wouldn't be so bad if this woman didn't charge so much a sandwich. I have a new route tomorrow, maybe it'll be better.*
> *I can't think of anything to write. A mental block.*
> *I keep finding goodies under my doorway that Rex*

keeps leaving me. Today it was a map to the stars' homes,
before it was books and a film directory and a variety of
Rex Roberts advertising. I think he's trying to make me.
I think I'll read. Shogun *is really a great book.*

For two wearisome, humiliating weeks, I sold sandwiches on a
route in Brentwood. Each morning I'd pick up a big, heavy wick-
er basket filled with overly-expensive, all-natural, slightly foul-
tasting concoctions in pita bread from a bakery in Westwood.
Half the people who reluctantly bought them took one bite and
wanted me to give them their money back, something that I had
been expressly forbidden from ever doing. This policy nearly got
me into at least one fight a day, and I always gave in and re-
funded their money before violence erupted. When I returned to
the bakery at the end of the day with several sandwiches each
with one bite out of them, I got yelled at, and was threatened
with having to pay for them myself. It was a completely unten-
able situation.

AUGUST 16, 1976
In one half of an hour I will be eighteen years old and
it really doesn't seem to mean a thing. I'm here by myself
in my little apartment. If I were in Michigan where the
drinking age is eighteen maybe it would matter. But here
in California where it's twenty-one, no.
Quit work today and Liz at the bakery made me feel
guilty. She didn't really make me, I made myself, neverthe-
less I feel guilty. Her sandwiches were terrible!
Re-wrote my story "Expectations" and mailed it away
to Alfred Hitchcock's Magazine. *I'm not very optimis-*
tic, but then I never am. For good reason, too, since I've
already had stories rejected by Argosy, Analog, Isaac
Asimov's Science Fiction Magazine, Galaxy, The New
Yorker, Penthouse *and* Playboy. *The most recent rejection*
came from Galaxy Science Fiction Magazine, *where I'd*
sent "The Sins of Space." Written on the cover page of the
story were these words, "Give me a break!" It was dif-
ficult to construe that as encouragement.
Meanwhile, I blew $19 today on assorted bullshit that

seems like a waste but I suppose it wasn't. This ribbon for instance, and this paper, both of which function correctly, as opposed to that Bargain Circus bullshit.

My next job was reading to, and typing for, a blind, overweight Latino man named Tony living in the odd, seemingly forgotten neighborhood of Palms. Tony was incredibly nice, had creepy blind white eyes, didn't smell very good, and was always covered in crumbs and food stains.

"How fast do you type?" asked Tony, waddling across the room, reaching from counter to chair to couch.

I sat before an IBM Selectric typewriter at a small, unstable metal typing desk.

"Uh, not that fast, really."

"Are you accurate?" asked Tony.

"Sometimes."

Tony handed me a piece of paper covered with type. "Hopefully, this will be one of those times. Here, retype this. You've got three minutes. Go."

I began typing, and sweating. I didn't even use all of my fingers to type—just my index fingers, and sometimes a thumb. I made a mistake and there was no correction key or white-out. Oh, shit! The only thing I had going for me was that Tony was blind and might not notice.

He noticed, or he gave it to someone who noticed for him. Tony did like the way I read, though, and kept me around for a while because of it. He had me bring in a few of my own stories and read them aloud. It was an illuminating, somewhat terrifying, experience.

Afterward, as I mopped my sweaty brow, Tony said, "Not bad. But you need to pay more attention to your prose. It's not as important in a screenplay, but in a short story or a novel it's crucial."

Sadly, after two weeks, my typing simply wasn't good enough, nor could I take dictation, so Tony had to let me go.

"Good luck," said Tony, shaking my hand with both of his chubby, sweaty hands. "And keep at it."

"I will, and thanks."

Next, I got a job selling office supplies over the telephone. I worked in a "boiler room" with 20 other people, all on telephones in little stalls filled with flashing, multi-line phones, and mountains of phone books from all over the country. What they had going on there was a very simple, old-fashioned hustle. You called any-one anywhere, although businesses were best, and you sold them Scotch tape and Bic pens at low prices, then you shipped them Nashua tape and no-brand pens. So, basically, you spent all day on the phone lying. I never for one second got used to hearing my-self say shit like, "So, you usin' a lot of that Scotch tape, are you?" or "Go through a lot of those Bic pens, do you?"

I lasted one week at minimum wage. The second week when they tried to switch me over to 100 percent commission, I quit.

The business's owner, a muscular blond surfer dude in his 30s, pointed in my face and stated, "You don't have what it takes, man! You'll never make it out here!"

I was aghast. "Oh, yeah? You tell people they're getting Bic pens and Scotch tape, then you send them crap! You're a liar and a cheat!"

The muscular surfer dude started to step out from behind the counter, "Oh, yeah? That's what it takes to make it out here, man! You got a problem with that?"

I backed up toward the door. "No, no problem." I got while the getting was good.

I walked west along Melrose past the long tan stucco walls of Paramount Pictures, thinking, "How the hell do I get in there?"

At the corner of Melrose and Gower Street, on the top corner of the soundstage was a big globe built right into the building. This was the original location of RKO-Radio Pictures, and once upon a time there had been a radio tower on top of the globe, forming the RKO logo. I looked up at the globe as I turned the corner, imagin-ing the radio tower on top of it, and thinking, "This is where they made *King Kong* and *Top Hat*, for Christ's sake."

I turned right on Gower, walking along past the many entrances to Paramount Pictures, then past the Hollywood Cemetery. Cross-ing Santa Monica Boulevard, I then passed Columbia Pictures which had been located there on Gower Street since 1924, right beside what used to be Poverty Row, the location of all the really,

really low-budget studios. Columbia had once been one of those really low-budget studios, up until they hired Frank Capra, that is—then their fortunes skyrocketed. The Three Stooges had shot all of their shorts there, too.

However, one day as I walked by, Columbia Pictures had mysteriously disappeared. I stopped and looked around. The main sign over the door was gone, as well as all references to it ever having been Columbia Pictures.

"Holy shit, Columbia's gone!"

On either side of Columbia's front doors there had been two black marble bas-reliefs of Harry and Joe Cohen, the founders of the studio, which I had stopped and looked at many times. But as I stood there now I saw that both reliefs were gone, leaving discolored squares on the stucco walls. I went inside and asked the middle-aged, bored, black security guard, "What happened to the plaques of Harry and Joe Cohen that were outside the doors?"

"Oh," said the guard, "they threw those out. Columbia moved out to Burbank, y'know."

I shook my head sadly. "Really? I didn't know. But they couldn't have taken the plaques with them?"

The guard shrugged, and harrumphed, indicating very clearly, who cares?

I walked away down Gower Street feeling depressed. I mumbled to myself, "Man, they don't give a shit about anything out here."

But that wasn't the end of it. On another day soon thereafter, as I drove down Washington Boulevard in Culver City, past the front of MGM studio, I saw a crane hoist away the big old neon-lighted MGM sign, with Leo the lion above the slogan *"Ars Gratia Artes,"* meaning "Art for Art's Sake." Right, like that was *ever* why MGM made a movie. The crane set the sign on the back of truck, no doubt to be taken to the garbage dump and scrapped. Soon it was replaced by a characterless black and white sign that said "Lorimar TelePictures."

As I drove by I said disdainfully, *"TelePictures?* Who gives a shit about telepictures? Oh, man, I got out here too late."

I began taking walks of three, four, and five miles around Hollywood. I ventured down nearly every street and alley in all directions within a two-mile radius of my apartment. I also began taking long stoned walks in the middle of the night, mainly just because I could, because there was nobody to tell me no.

Hollywood was truly a shit-hole, particularly east of Vine, where my street, Van Ness, happened to be located. But West Hollywood wasn't much better. Hookers lined both sides of Sunset Boulevard from Western Avenue all the way through Hollywood, along the Sunset Strip, right through West Hollywood, and directly up to the edge of Beverly Hills. Three or four miles of hookers, literally hundreds of them, maybe thousands, exclusively black and Latino at the eastern end, then as you traveled west they got progressively more attractive, with white girls joining in somewhere in the middle of Hollywood. By the time you got to the Sunset Strip the girls were absolutely gorgeous, of every race, creed and color, and mostly attired in colorful, form-fitting, one-piece Danskin bathing suits, stockings and high heels. As I walked along Sunset Boulevard I always eyed the girls longingly—if I only had the money, man oh man . . .

An incredibly curvaceous black hooker in a red bathing suit asked, "Hey, honey, wanna date?"

I sighed. "I wish. Would you take an IOU?"

She grinned. "Yeah, you *wish*."

Meanwhile, male hustlers lined both sides of Santa Monica Boulevard all the way through West Hollywood for more than a mile. I found walking up either Sunset or Santa Monica boulevards such an ordeal of being accosted and propositioned that I generally avoided both of them, taking De Longpre or Fountain instead when going east or west.

Hollywood Boulevard, on the other hand, particularly after midnight, became my favorite haunt. I'd wear a baggy army jacket with a knife in my pocket, just in case. Looking like some sort of psycho, I would walk over the slick gray terrazzo surface of Hollywood Boulevard, on top of the slippery pink stars with the names of movie actors, directors, producers, and even the occasional cartoon character, animal, or rock band emblazoned upon them. I thought, "One day I'll have a star on Hollywood Boulevard."

In the middle of the night on the boulevard there'd be the occasional ugly hooker, but for the most part it was pretty much exclusively crazy people, homeless people, drug addicts, and bewildered-looking musicians wearing colorful Spandex pants, pointy boots, and carrying electric guitars over their shoulders—the flotsam and jetsam of Hollywood.

I was drawn to all of this, and actually sort of reveled in it, but I never felt like I was a part of it. I was just an observer, a writer attempting to pass as one of them to gather material—it was all research. Like Gregory Peck passing as a Jew in *Gentleman's Agreement*. But way deep down I also feared that if things didn't work out in the film business, which they often hadn't for many people in the past, I could become one of these denizens of the street for real. One more movie writer-director who failed, cracked up, became an alcoholic, and now wanders up and down Hollywood Boulevard late at night howling at the moon. I could see it—I was being played by Humphrey Bogart, a cigarette dangling from the corner of my mouth, with Gloria Grahame as the dame.

It was a possibility, of course, but not very likely. I was going to make it. I was going to be a writer-director; that was for sure. How far I'd ascend within that realm, well, that remained to be seen. But I just knew I'd go all the way to the top. I'd get up there with Hitchcock and Ford. Not right away, of course, but eventually. It had to be. It was written. Although, for some men truly nothing is written.

I pointed at my temple, "It's written in here."

And while I walked I thought. "What stories are worth telling? What stories do *I* need to tell? Have I ever done anything in my life that was worthy of being a movie? I mean, where do stories come from, anyway?"

"Hey, man, can ya spare some change?"

I would just ignore the panhandlers like they didn't exist. Sometimes I enjoyed pretending that I was insane, a Vietnam vet with post-traumatic stress disorder seething with anger and ready to explode. Just like Travis Bickle in *Taxi Driver*, but instead of a .44 Magnum, I had a Buck knife in my pocket that I'd gotten from my parents as a Bar Mitzvah present with my initials engraved on it (just in case I ever had to use it as murder weapon it could be easily identified as mine).

Deep down I was angry, too. Why did my dad treat me like such a jerk? Didn't he see this was what I had to do? What I was meant to do? That this was my destiny?

No. Dad thought I should stay at Michigan. What he didn't realize was that just wasn't humanly possible for me. I'd managed to go from a 4.0 and on the dean's list at Oakland Community College, to a 3.0 at Eastern Michigan University, to a 1.9 at the University of Michigan. I really could've stayed at Eastern, but Dad was the one who advised me to go to Michigan when I finally got accepted halfway through the semester. Dad said, "You get accepted to U of M, you go to U of M." I couldn't deny his logic, but the fact was that I had just turned 17 years old and realistically should have been in 12ᵗʰ grade. I mean, I'd handled community college—4.0 and the dean's list—and I could even handle EMU—3.0 was perfectly acceptable, if not impressive—but U of M was immediately and totally over my immature 17-year-old head. As soon as I realized that my being there at U of M was a disaster, like one week in, I began making plans to bail out to Hollywood.

Dad was totally against me going to Hollywood. Not that it mattered, but it still pissed me off.

"You could try be supportive, y'know," I said aloud.

A homeless man going the other way said, "What?"

I shook my head, "Never mind."

Every night I'd pass the Scientology Center on Hollywood Boulevard where there was always a guy out front hawking their wares and trying to get the passersby to take an E-Meter test. "Improve your life, improve your marriage, improve your memory . . ." Night after night this same Scientologist accosted me every single time I walked by. Finally, I'd had enough. I stopped and confronted the guy.

"Does it really and truly improve your memory?"

"Yes, it does," stated the Scientologist categorically.

"Then remember my face and never bother me again."

The next night, as I walked by, the same guy accosted me.

"Take an E-Meter test?"

I stopped. "Do you remember me?"

The guy looked straight at me. "No."

"Just as I suspected." I pointed in the Scientologist's face. "You, sir, and your entire organization are a sham!"

The brainwashed Scientologist turned away and was already pestering the next pedestrian. Sure, I was just one more nutball wandering up and down Hollywood Boulevard in the middle of the night, but as I walked on I felt vindicated that at least for the moment I hadn't yet fallen for that level of foolishness.

At the western end of Hollywood Boulevard just down from the Chinese Theater was the Nagoya Massage. It was one of the very few businesses on the boulevard open all night. The front of the establishment was no more than a neon-lighted doorway. But a doorway leading to what? Ah, *that* was the question.

Leafing through the L.A. Weekly, I spotted a Nagoya Massage $10 off introductory coupon, with photos of pretty topless Oriental girls in the ad. I quickly tore out the coupon and put in my wallet. So now each night as I walked by Nagoya Massage, I could feel my wallet in my back pocket burning my ass.

Since I had managed in my first few months in Hollywood to not make any friends, I was growing incredibly, seriously, cosmically lonely.

So, as I walked past Nagoya Massage for about the 30th time, I finally summoned up all my nerve, opened the door and went in. I strode purposefully up to the middle-aged Asian woman behind the desk and presented the coupon.

"Here," I said.

"Give that to girl after. Room three."

She buzzed a door leading further inside. I thought, "Holy shit, is that it?" I nervously went through the door.

I walked down a hallway with numbered doors on one side. I stopped in front of the door marked 3, slowly turned the knob, opened the door and went in. There was a cushioned massage table and a pile of towels, and other than that it was empty and clean. I sat down on the table.

A few minutes later a ridiculously cute slim little Asian "masseuse" with bangs straight across her forehead, wearing just a robe, entered the room and shut the door. "You very young," she observed.

"I'm 21," I said.

"Sure you are. Me, too. You take off all your clothes, okay? I be right back."

She left the room and I hesitantly took of my clothes. I wasn't sure what to do with my wallet, so I left it in my pants' pocket, then wound the rest of my clothes up around it. I stripped down to my underwear and sat down on the massage table.

After what seemed like a half an hour, but was really about 10 minutes, the girl returned. She closed the door, pointed at my underwear, and said, "You take those off, too, okay?"

I said, "Okay."

I removed my underwear revealing my woody. I looked up blushing.

The girl smiled. "Oh, you already hard. That's very good. You lie down, okay?" She pushed me back until I was lying down on the table.

Once I was on my back, my dick was sticking straight up in the air. The Asian girl squirted oil on her hand, then took a firm hold of me and began to vigorously jack me off. It felt wonderful and I closed my eyes.

"You just relax."

I relaxed, reached up under the girl's robe, taking hold of her round little ass cheek, feeling the warmth up between her legs, then I immediately came. She continued jacking me off for another minute until she was sure I was completely done, then she took a handful of tissues and expertly cleaned me up.

"That was good, huh?"

I sighed and nodded, "Yeah, it was."

"You come back, okay? You ask for me. I'm Alice."

"Okay, Alice."

"We can do other things, too. For more money."

"Right."

I presented Alice with my coupon, then only had to pay $15 more. It seemed worth it, too, even if it only took about 60 seconds. But at least it wasn't me doing it to myself. And man was she cute!

I walked up the boulevard feeling relieved, my hands in my pockets and a crooked grin on my face.

"Other things, eh? What other things? And how much?"

My next stupid job was in a big old bookstore that specialized in oversized art books and was located right near the L.A. airport. Jets went over all day long coming in so low on their approach to the airport that they seemed like they were going to land right on the bookstore's roof. The store was obviously on its way out of business at some point in the very near future and was owned by a crazy old man. The other two employees were a middle-aged Latino woman and her 15-year-old son. The crazy old store owner demanded that all of the oversized art books be wrapped in big sheets of Saran Wrap, as though they were brand new and had just come from the factory. When anyone actually wanted to look through one of the books, they would invariably become all confused and flustered and ask if it was okay to tear off the wrapping. Sure. They'd then tear off all the Saran Wrap and discard it, glance through the book, then set it aside and go unwrap and glance at another book. It was the responsibility of the three employees to run around after them picking up cantaloupe-sized wads of plastic wrap, as well as all of the now-unwrapped books that were left behind, and then begin the endless process of rewrapping them. This insane job lasted two ridiculously long, monotonous weeks.

I then got a job as cashier at Shep's Deli on Pico Boulevard, not too far from 20th Century Fox Studios. This was the least offensive of all the crummy jobs I'd had so far, so I just stuck with it. Brian Wilson from The Beach Boys was a regular lunch customer. Wilson had clearly had a severe nervous breakdown and was always accompanied by a short, loud psychiatrist. Brian was bearded, overweight, and easily confused, but very pleasant in his own dopey way. After each enormous lunch of a couple of corned beef sandwiches, Brian would sign the credit card slip in his utterly psychotic, illegible scrawl. After he left, several of the waitresses and cooks would come by and check out his signature, saying things like, "Man, he's fucked up."

Lindsey Buckingham from Fleetwood Mac, who couldn't be more popular, had lunch there a few times, but not too many people knew who he was, even though he had enormous hair. Farrah Fawcett came in once looking very attractive. She was a huge star in the hit TV show *Charlie's Angels* at that time, and her presence caused a real commotion. She ordered a pound of sliced turkey and a rye bread to go. In one second there were 20 people standing around her. Meanwhile, *Charlie's Angels* had been on the night before, and Bud, the short, fat deli man from Brooklyn, said, "You were very good last night."

Farrah Fawcett smiled and said, "Thank you."

Everybody standing around was momentarily stunned. Did he mean what it sounded like? Then everyone burst out laughing.

Because I didn't mind waking up early, I always took the morning breakfast shift, starting at 7:00 A.M. However, in the mornings I had to be both cashier and deli man until Bud wandered in around 10:00. The problems with this were twofold: one, there was no good way to get from the cash register to behind the deli counter without having to go all the way down to the other end of the deli counter, which was like 100 feet long, go around behind, then come all the way back down to where the rye bread and lunch meats were kept; and two, I didn't like using the bread-cutting machine or the meat-slicing machine. Since I'd never been particularly coordinated to start with, I was always pretty certain I was just about to chop off one of my fingers. Invariably, right when I had to use one of these deadly machines, someone would step up to the cash register to pay their bill. I would then have to run the length of the deli counter, come around the corner, run the length again, go behind the register and ring up the sale. Then the cutting or slicing machine would finish its business and I'd have to run back. It was an unworkable system, particularly when there were people lined up in both places. Several times I did not set the machines correctly, and turned them on and ran away, only to witness the machines either squash and shred an entire loaf of rye bread or fling a three-pound hunk of meat on the floor.

> *SEPTEMBER 27, 1976*
>
> *I have not made an entry in the journal for several weeks, maybe months, but now I shall.*
>
> *I'm feeling kind of low in myself. Not real low, just kind of. For instance I have to be up at 6:00 tomorrow to go to work at the deli. It doesn't seem too bad, but it ain't great. One waitress is pretty good looking, but not great. Kind of like Kathy on* Mary Hartman, Mary Hartman.
>
> *I really think I should be a nervous wreck, so far it's just a minor collision.*
>
> *I'm lonely. Really lonely. I can't even keep up with writing. I suppose complaining won't help, but it doesn't seem to hurt and I haven't anything better to do. I can't go back*

to Detroit, but things don't seem to be working out here. Maybe I should move out of this crazy faggot building. I don't know.

Across the hall and to the right, in apartment number 9, lived an obese black man named Nate who was a drunk. He was friends with an old homeless drunk man named Bob who lived in the parking lot across the street. Bob and Nate would often sit in Nate's 1965 Rambler wagon in front of the building listening to the ball game on the radio while drinking all day and all night. I thought, "Bob was probably around for the golden age of Hollywood, but he was so smash-assed drunk in that parking lot he missed it."

I would also think about the landlord Dan's comment about "fuckin' faggots, big ones, little ones, fat ones, skinny ones, black ones, white ones." Did that mean that 350-pound Nate was gay and having sex with old, homeless Bob? Somehow my 18-year-old mind couldn't fathom such a thing.

One rainy night there was a knock at my door and it was Nate.

"You wanna make $20?"

I said suspiciously, "What d'ya mean?"

"That's your yellow wagon, right?"

"Yeah."

"You need to take two people downtown, then bring 'em back."

"What for?"

"For 20 bucks, that's what for."

As my mouth said, "Okay," my brain said, "*Hey, asshole!* Maybe you should try thinking about things a bit longer before answering."

I wasn't even sure if Nate would fit into the passenger seat of my little wagon. The whole car creaked and tilted to the right. Nate had me stop my car in front of a building about a block away. Nate went in, then came out a few minutes later with two white guys in their 20s who were completely stoned on heroin. Nate came around to the driver's window and I lowered it.

"Just take 'em where they tell ya," said Nate, handing me a moist, crumpled-up, worn-out, 20-dollar bill that I hesitantly took. Nate turned and waddled away up the sidewalk.

I now fully realized what was going on—I was about to drive these two junkies from Hollywood to downtown L.A. in the rain to score heroin. This seemed like a really foolish way to make 20 bucks.

"Go downtown," slurred one of the junkies.

I said, "I'll take the freeway, okay?"

"Sure, take the freeway. I'll tell ya when to get off."

I watched in my rearview mirror as one of the junkies holding a plastic container kept unsteadily scooping up big globs of tuna salad on a fork, bringing it up near his mouth, then more times than not losing it somewhere in my backseat. I found this so distracting that as I drove down the Hollywood Freeway my eyes began crossing between the road ahead and the mess occurring behind me.

Then neither junkie really knew which exit to take.

"Get off at Spring Street."

"No, Hope Street."

"We passed Hope."

"Then Spring."

"It's coming up."

I got off at Spring Street.

"Turn here."

I turned.

"No, turn here."

I turned.

I had no idea where I was as I drove around one corner after another after another in funky, low-budget, entirely black and Latino downtown L.A. in the rain. Finally, the junkies saw someone on a corner and yelled, "Stop here!"

I stopped in the middle of the street and both junkies ran out into the rain, disappearing into the night. I didn't know what to do next. I circled the block a few times thinking, "How long am I supposed to wait? At what point do I abandon them for dead?" And it seemed that every other car I passed was a slow-moving black and white L.A. police cruiser.

Like zombies in a horror movie, the two junkies came running back out of the rainy night and banged on my car windows. I gasped in fright. The junkies got into the car, soaking wet, but victorious. I then proceeded to drive them back home. I was so freaked out and turned around backward that I didn't even try to find the freeway entrance. Instead, when I finally saw a street I recognized, Melrose, I got on it and took it all the way back. Since this route took longer, and with no time to wait, both junkies decided to run up the heroin in the car. I couldn't believe what I was seeing in my rearview mirror—they were cooking heroin in a spoon with a match, then filling a syringe and sticking it into their arms. I began mumbling to himself, "Oh my God, oh my God . . ."

I finally pulled up in front of their building, stopped the car, lowered my head to the steering wheel and took a deep breath.

"Okay, here we are."

Both junkies were so wasted they didn't move. They both looked dead.

I got out of the car, opened the back door, pulled one of them out, put the guy's arm around my neck, and pretty much carried him into the building.

I asked, "Which apartment do you live in?"

"Huh?"

"Which apartment?"

He'd nodded back out.

"*Holy fuck!*"

Luckily, the door to one apartment was open and loud music was coming out. Also, two female junkies were eagerly awaiting the male junkie's return. The girls came out and helped bring the guy in. I went back outside for the other one, and one of the girls came and assisted. I looked at the junkie girl and thought, "She might actually be cute, if she didn't look dead." We got the other guy inside, then I hastily split.

When I got back into my car I looked in the backseat and it was completely covered with tuna salad, as well as the plastic container and the fork, and the little paper wrappers that the heroin came in. The car was going to have to be hosed out.

I took the 20-dollar bill out of my pocket and inspected it. It looked like somebody had wiped their ass with it. "Fuck! I'm such an idiot!"

I took my hard-earned money and went home.

OCTOBER 4, 1976
The whole cast and crew of Police Story *is having lunch right across the street in the parking lot of the Encore Theater. There are trucks, buses, police cars (that don't really look like police cars), police motorcycles (that don't look*

real because six real LAPD drove up and are having a free lunch with the cast). It's interesting, but no filming is going on, just lunch. It sure must cost a bundle to film something like this. There have to be 50 or 60 people eating lunch. Think of the food bills alone.

Two of the real cops just pulled out, they must have finished eating. Lou, the owner of the Encore, just pulled out and waved to me. The cops just pulled back in, for dessert maybe.

Fake cops mingling with real cops, all eating a buffet style lunch.

Everyone is either in a police uniform (it's very easy to tell the real ones from the actors) or wearing a funny hat. The star, whatever-his-name-may-be, just walked by, and someone ran up and joined him. You don't walk alone if you're a star. Even on a TV show.

I think lunch is over. Everyone is clinging to a script bound in a blue cover. An old man is wheeling out a wooden box. Cars are pulling out and a tow truck pulled up.

Everything is pulling out. I think they're filming at the school up the street.

I sat at my typewriter pecking away when there was a knock on the door behind me. Odd, I wasn't expecting anyone. I opened the door and there stood my old girlfriend from junior high school, Leigh Albertson, holding a suitcase. She was as beautiful as ever, slim, petite, dark wavy hair, but most impressive were her unusually big wide eyes—turquoise with flecks of yellow in them. They were cat eyes. Crazy eyes.

I was astounded. "Leigh. What are you doing here?"

"Can I come in?"

"Of course. Come in."

Leigh came in and looked around the tiny apartment.

"This is cute."

"Thanks. Sixty-five dollars a month, including utilities. And I'm right across the street from Paramount Pictures."

Leigh set down her suitcase, took off her coat and sat on the third-of-a-couch. "Impressive."

I asked, "Would you like a cup of coffee?"

Leigh said, "Sure."

I put the kettle on the hotplate. I sat down on the day-glo orange imitation chair, hurting my tailbone on the particle board cushion as I always did.

"So, not to pry or anything, but what are you doing here in L.A.?"

Leigh said, "I'll take the coffee first, okay?"

"Sure." I lit a cigarette. "Want one?"

"Okay." Leigh took a cigarette and I lit it for her. She held it and smoked it like she didn't really smoke. I couldn't remember her ever smoking.

I said, "So, when was the last time we saw each other? At U of M, right?"

"I guess so."

"You cooked fish and burned it, then we went out to dinner, remember?"

Leigh's big eyes watched the smoke swirl upward off the end of the cigarette. "Uh-huh," she answered absently.

We both sat silently smoking for a long uncomfortable moment, then the kettle thankfully whistled. I jumped to my feet. "Okay then." I took the kettle off the hotplate and asked, "Milk? Sugar?"

"Black, thanks."

I made two cups of instant coffee, using three spoonfuls of coffee in each cup. I added milk and sugar to my own, then turned and handed the cup of black coffee to Leigh. I sat back down on the orange chair and hurt my ass again.

"So, not to press the point, but what brings you to L.A.?"

Leigh took a sip of her coffee. "Mmmm, good. Uh, well . . ." She took a puff of the cigarette, but didn't inhale. "I was having some troubles, so I took a trip around the world, and now I'm on my way home."

"Uh-huh?"

"Uh-huh, what?"

I didn't know where to start. "Well, what kind of troubles?"

"Oh, I tried to kill myself. It wasn't the first time."

"Oh." I didn't know what to say.

Leigh sipped her coffee. "Yeah."

After another long awkward pause, I asked, "So, do you have to get back to the airport tonight, or are you staying here in L.A.?"

Leigh turned her intense, wide-eyed, pleading gaze upon him. "I was hoping I could stay here with you for a while."

"For a while?"

"A few days?"

I nodded. "Sure."

"On the couch."

I laughed.

"What's so funny?" asked Leigh.

"I've only got a third of a couch, and you're sitting on it. I think it's too small for even you to sleep on. But we'll work something out. I have a sleeping bag."

"Thank you."

"No problem. There's a cool Mexican joint just up the street called Lucy's. We can go there for dinner if you'd like."

"That would be great."

Leigh and I had dinner at Lucy's, and we both had a few margaritas. After dinner we walked around the neighborhood smoking cigarettes. As we approached the Encore Theater, I told Leigh about my adventures there in the projection booth, and back at Lou's place. Just as we passed the theater, there stood Lou smoking a cigarette. I waved.

"Hello, Lou."

Lou waved back. "Hello, Josh. Is that your girlfriend?"

I took Leigh's arm. "She's my *old* girlfriend."

"She don't look too old to me," he laughed lasciviously, then began to cough and spat on the sidewalk.

Leigh smiled, putting her hand on mine. "What a cozy neighborhood."

I laughed. "Yeah, for a ghetto."

We watched TV and took turns taking showers. Then it was time for bed.

I said, "I'll take the sleeping bag, you take the bed."

Leigh said, "No. Uh-uh. I'll take the sleeping bag, you sleep in your own bed. I'm the one who just showed up unannounced. I'm not putting you out of your bed, too."

"That's okay, I don't mind."

"No, it's not okay with me."

Etc.

Leigh won and I got the bed. Leigh curled up in the sleeping bag on the thin worn carpet on the hard floor. I put out the light, then pretty promptly fell asleep.

However, at some unspecified point during the night, Leigh crawled up into bed with me.

"It's too uncomfortable on the floor," said Leigh, curling up against my back.

I turned around and took Leigh's hand in mine.

Leigh quickly said, "We can fool around, but I don't want to have sex."

"Why not?"

"'Cause I don't, that's why."

"Okay."

I kissed her, and she absently kissed me back. I pulled her slim, small-breasted somewhat bony body against mine so she could feel the full extent of my big throbbing woody, but it didn't seem to matter. After a few minutes she turned away and feigned sleep. I lay there on my side, my dick ridiculously hard and snuggled up between the cheeks of her cute little butt. I continued to stroke her arm and kiss the back of her neck.

She finally pushed me away and whispered, "Go to sleep."

I rolled over so my woody was no longer touching her. I desperately wanted to jerk off, or at least have a cigarette. But instead I just lay there quietly, trying not to move, waiting to hear or sense that Leigh had fallen asleep.

I whispered softly, "I understood when we first went out in junior high and you wouldn't let me even get to second base, let alone actually have sex with me. But Leigh, I saw you at a party during high school. It was at somebody's house with a pool and everybody was taking 'ludes. You certainly were, though I didn't. But first I saw you in the bushes actually having sex with one guy, then later with another guy, then later with yet another guy. Okay, that was a drug-addled night in high school. But why won't you have sex with *me*? I really like you and always have. What's this all about?"

Leigh turned around and took my hands in hers. She opened her big crazy turquoise eyes wide and said, "*I don't know. I don't know what's wrong with me. I'm a severely fucked-up mess. Okay?*"

I nodded. "Okay then."

"Good." She turned over.

I turned over, too. We each got as far away from each other as we could on a single bed, although our bottoms still just barely touched.

Thankfully, at some point we both fell asleep.

Leigh stayed for two more days. The longer she was there, the stranger she seemed to get, and the more tense the atmosphere grew. We didn't kiss or fool around or anything anymore; we just slept in the same little bed. I really wanted to fuck her brains out, but her brain already seemed too scrambled. Nor did we ever have an entire conversation, either. Partway through Leigh would always fade away somewhere, her big eyes wandering off unfocused toward the ceiling.

Leigh and I walked along Hollywood Boulevard. Leigh had her 35mm camera and insisted on taking a photograph of every single star on the sidewalk, no matter who they were, and there are hundreds of them.

"Leigh," I said. "You don't even know who Olive Borden is, and neither do I."

Leigh got down on her hands and knees and picked a wad of dried bubblegum off the star with her thumbnail. She then stood, focused and took another picture.

Four more steps, then she stopped to photograph the next star, "Mark Serrurier, Inventor of the Moviola." Leigh kicked away the candy wrappers, focused, and shot. I stood and smoked a cigarette watching Leigh busily and obsessively creep her way up the boulevard. And she seemed to have plenty of film, too. She stopped and reloaded a few times.

I thought, "This will be the dullest series of photographs ever taken in Hollywood, and that's saying something."

After more than an hour of this lunacy, and possibly a hundred photographs, I'd had enough. I flicked my cigarette butt, firmly grabbed Leigh's thin bony arm, and physically led her off the boulevard and onto a side street. Leigh seemed completely confused.

"What's going on?"

"Leigh, the stars on Hollywood Boulevard go on for over a mile. Let's go have some lunch. I'm starving."

Leigh kept turning around like she really wanted to go back and keep shooting, but I kept my hand on her arm and led her directly into the nearest restaurant.

Later that day, I found myself sitting down in the fucked-up basement of the apartment building washing my clothes and reading a book, not wanting to go back up to my own apartment because Leigh was there. Sadly, she was just too weird to deal with.

I looked up from my book, remembering a winter afternoon in junior high, back when Leigh and I were going out. Big fluffy snowflakes floated down from the sky like feathers. It wasn't very cold, and deep crunchy snow covered the ground. Leigh was wearing a fur coat made of some sort of long soft blonde fur, as well as fur boots, and she looked absolutely gorgeous. She and I walked through the snow with our arms around each other, not talking, crunching along, step by step. We sat down on a cold stone bench in somebody's backyard. After a moment of watching the snowflakes float down, we slowly kissed very softly, barely touching lips.

It was magical, like being in Fairyland with a beautiful snow princess. I was utterly enchanted. Possibly even in love.

Thunk! The dryer in the filthy basement at 666 North Van Ness turned off, wrenching me back to my ugly reality.

On the day of her flight, Leigh wouldn't let me drive her to the airport.

"You can just drop me off at the Hotel Roosevelt on Hollywood Boulevard. I'll catch a bus to the airport from there."

I repeated over and over, "Leigh, I don't mind driving you to the airport. It's not really all that far."

Leigh wouldn't hear of it. "No, no, no. I've tried your patience and your good will more than enough. Just drop me at the Hotel Roosevelt. It's not that far, right?"

"No, it's not."

"Good."

So I took her to the Hotel Roosevelt. I pulled over to the side of Orange Drive, right across from the hotel, and stopped the car. We sat in silence for a long moment.

Finally, I said, "The very first Oscar ceremony was held here at the Hotel Roosevelt in 1929."

Leigh said, "I'm sorry I annoyed you so badly, and wouldn't

have sex with you, either."

I shrugged. "That's okay, Leigh. It was good seeing you."

"Oh, sure."

"It was. You're as beautiful as ever."

"I probably should've had sex with you."

I pointed at the car's clock and grinned. "I'll bet there's still time before your flight, if you let me drive you to the airport."

"No, no, I've got to go."

I snapped my fingers. "Oh, well. It was worth a try."

Leigh suddenly looked like she was going to cry. I smiled weakly.

"I was just kidding."

Leigh nodded. "I know." She turned and looked straight at me with her big crazy cat eyes, helplessly, pleading.

I said, "What?"

Leigh looked like she was going to say something, then didn't. She shook her head and opened the door.

"Goodbye, Josh."

"Goodbye, Leigh."

I took hold of her thin bicep, pulled her to me and gave her a kiss. It was like kissing someone who was anesthetized.

Leigh got out of the car, opened the back door, took out her suitcase and crossed the street to the hotel. I sat there watching her go into the hotel. She came back out a minute later and stepped up to the bus stop at the curb on Hollywood Boulevard.

I drove up to the light and made a right onto Hollywood Boulevard, in front of the Chinese Theater. Glancing up into my rearview mirror, I could see Leigh's lonely little figure standing all by herself at the curb with her suitcase waiting for the bus.

I sighed, "Leigh."

OCTOBER 13, 1976

I have just gotten very high. I smoked a small chunk of Thai stick and got tied. Tide, maybe? Who knows.

It's difficult typing this high.

In exactly four hours I have to be at work.

I wonder how fast Kurt Vonnegut can type. Probably much faster than me. Who cares?

I've been keeping this journal pretty regularly now, and

I really wonder what the point is. It keeps me writing,
anyway.
   Reflected image on the glass, inside, outside and me."

Right outside my window was the fire escape, and where I kept
my one spindly ficus plant I'd gotten as a present from my sister.
As I stood out on the fire escape in my bathrobe watering the
plant, I looked down and saw a very pretty, slim, black girl, who
sort of resembled a young Leslie Uggams, wearing a tight-fitting
shiny turquoise leotard top and jeans, moving her boxes into the
building. I looked up to the heavens and said, "Thank you, Lord,"
then promptly popped a big woody that came right out the front
of my bathrobe.

"*Whoops!*"

I climbed in the window, ran over to the door, opened it an inch,
and peered out. The gorgeous girl was moving her stuff into apartment seven, right across the hall. Oh, yeah! I quickly got dressed
and ran down the stairs. Slowing to an unhurried walk as I passed
her in the foyer, I casually asked . . .

"Need any help?"

Her pretty face lit up into an even prettier smile. "Sure. That'd
be great. If it's not a problem."

I shook my head. "No. No problem at all." I put out my hand.
"Hi, I'm Josh Becker. I'm in apartment 6."

She shook my hand. Her hand was small and rough. "Kerrie
Kettering. I don't remember my apartment number."

I said, "Seven. You're right across the hall from me."

Kerrie immediately looked suspicious, pulling her hand away.
"How do you know?"

I was taken aback by her abrupt attitude change. "Your door's
open. I just saw it when I came down."

Kerrie looked relieved, putting her hand directly upon her lus-
cious, small, clearly-defined breast. "Oh, right. Well, thanks, I sure
could use the help."

I helped her bring in all her stuff, which was hardly anything.
Once it was all inside, I backed slowly toward the door.

"Well, then, I guess that's everything."

Kerrie nodded. "Yeah. Thanks again."

"Okay then. See ya 'round. Neighbor."

She flashed her pretty smile at me. "You, too, neighbor."

I hesitantly left.

When I got back inside my own apartment I didn't know what to do. I finally sat down on the bed, undid my jeans, and let loose my raging boner. I closed my eyes and began masturbating.

Just then there was a knock at my door.

I panicked. "Who is it?"

"It's Kerrie. Can I come in?"

"One second." I hastily put my hard-on away, pulled up my pants, and fastened them. I jumped to my feet and casually opened the door.

"Hi."

"Am I disturbing you?"

"No, not at all. Come on in."

Kerrie held a brand new dead-bolt in the plastic package in her hand.

"Have you got any idea how to install one of these?"

I waved my hand at the door. "Sure. I installed my own."

Kerrie glanced down at my door and saw that my dead-bolt was crooked, and about as poorly installed as was humanly possible, with scratches and claw marks in the wood all around it.

I added, "I learned a lot from installing that one. I think I've got it now."

Kerrie asked sweetly, "Could you help me?"

I grinned. "I'd be happy to."

"You're so nice."

"Yeah."

Kerrie turned around, and headed back to her own apartment. As I stood up and took a step I could barely walk with my dick so hard and bent in the wrong position. I quickly rearranged my goods when she wasn't looking.

It took two hours for me to install the dead-bolt in Kerrie's door for her, and I did do a better job than on my own door. As Kerrie unloaded her boxes, and I installed the lock, we talked and talked.

Kerrie said, "I'm from New York. I've only been out in L.A. for six months. I want to be an actress."

I smiled, "How unique. Which restaurant do you work in?"

Kerrie grinned. "Actually, I'm working as a dancer in a club. Here."

She handed me a photo album. Every photograph was of her in a different nude pose. I took this as a positive sign. My cock was now exploding out of my pants and trying to strangle me.

I asked, "Wanna go out to eat?"

"Sure."

Having almost no money, I took Kerrie out to dinner at McDonald's. She wore a white fisherman's sweater and looked ridiculously attractive. She smelled of coconuts.

"I just split up with a guy," said Kerrie. "We'd been together a long time, like almost two years, and my heart's broken, okay? I'm definitely not looking to get involved in anything new this soon, that's for sure."

As I ate French fries and nodded understandingly, I thought, "Who's talking about getting involved? And what a *great* idea."

I said, "Yeah, my heart's broken, too. I left my girlfriend back in Detroit, and if you want to know the truth, I don't think she loves me anymore. She's sure not writing back to me anymore. Out of sight, out of mind. "

Kerrie nodded, reached out and touched my hand with her rough little hand. I melted. Coconuts.

When we got back to my apartment, I rolled a joint and we smoked it. As we sat close to each other on the third-of-a-sectional couch, I reached out, put my arm around her, pulled her to me, and kissed her lightly. And after a second her lips parted, allowing my tongue entrance into her warm waiting mouth. Her small rough hand took hold of my neck. We kissed energetically for a moment, then I put my hand on her breast and Kerrie suddenly pushed me away.

"No. This is too quick. Uh-uh."

I rolled my eyes, "Oh, come on."

"No, I just met you."

"So?"

Kerrie shook her head. "What kind of slut do you take me for?"

I grinned, "A pretty one?"

Kerrie pushed me hard in the chest.

"*Asshole!*"

I laughed and held up my open hands.

"Kidding. Joke."

Kerrie looked serious and asked, "You think I'm a slut?"

"No," I said seriously, then burst out laughing.

"What?"

"Well, I have already seen about 50 pictures of you naked."

"You think that means something?"

"No. I'm just kidding. Calm down."

Kerrie got to her feet. "Okay, Josh. It was nice meeting you."

"Very nice meeting you, too, Kerrie."

"Good night."

She opened the door, turned, gave me a cute smile and a little wave, then left.

I lit the roach and took a big hit. "Wow! And she lives right next door."

A few days later in the middle of the night, there was a knock at my door.

I woke up and looked at the clock. "What the hell? It's 3:00 A.M."

The door was located right at the foot of the bed, so I sat up, leaned forward and opened the door.

There stood Kerrie, entirely naked, silhouetted against the light in the hall.

"Can I come in?" she asked, rather demurely under the circumstances.

I grabbed Kerrie's hand and pulled her directly into bed.

"I thought you didn't want to get involved?"

Kerrie said, "I don't. I'm just going to use you, like a toy."

"Really?"

"Yeah, really. Have you ever slept with a black girl before?"

I shook my head. "No."

Kerrie grinned. "Then you're in for a treat."

I grinned back. "Oh, yeah?"

Kerrie's rough little hand reached down and grabbed a hold of my already rock hard woody, squeezing it with a firm grip. I gulped.

Kerrie said, "Yeah."

She rubbed herself against my leg, then slowly slid down my side and vigorously went down on me. In about 30 seconds it was too much for me.

"Holy shit!" I gasped. I was about to come already. "Stop, stop." I pulled out of her mouth.

She said, "What?"

"I was about to come."

"That's okay."

"Really?"

"Sure. Now you go down me."

I said, "Okay."

"Have you ever gone down on a girl before?"

"Yeah," I said, like I'd done it a hundred times, when in fact I'd done it just once, had absolutely no idea what I was doing, and had quickly stopped.

I slowly licked and kissed my way down her stomach, past her belly button, and to her full bush of curly black pubic hair—it was pungent and fishy and salty, intoxicating, and nearly overwhelming. Kerrie grabbed the back of my head and held on to my hair. I poked out my tongue and began licking.

Kerrie said, "Up . . . Higher . . . Up . . . Stop. Right there. Okay, faster, and no teeth."

I did as I was instructed. Kerrie began to moan, pushing my face harder into her crotch. I was beginning to have trouble breathing, but just kept on licking, and Kerrie kept moaning and sighing and pulling on the back of my head with all her strength.

But after a point her pleasured moans were making me crazy. I pulled my face up, wiped it off with my hand, dried it on her stomach, then found my way back up to her waiting mouth and kissed her. Her small rough hands took hold of me, guiding me inside of her. Kerrie gasped in my ear.

"Yeah, baby. You go for it. Go for *all* of it."

Coconuts. It was in her hair.

Luckily for me, having recently just teetered right on the edge of an orgasm, I was now able to control myself. I energetically fucked Kerrie for a few minutes. Kerrie grabbed my ass and hung on.

"Oh, yeah, baby. I knew you'd be good at this, I could just tell."

I was too busy kissing her neck and fucking her to answer. And in just a few more moments I came. It was like everything in my body rushed out of me in a tidal wave. Kerrie hastily pulled me out of her, grabbed some tissues, put them to her crotch, and dashed into the bathroom.

I just lay there on my side smelling the coconut oil on my pillow.

Kerrie called out from the bathroom, "I'm on the pill, by the way. Thanks for asking."

I sighed. "I meant to ask."

"Yeah, I'm sure you did."

I was sitting on the couch reading. There was a knock at the door and I called out, "It's open. Come on in."

Kerrie walked in attired in a tiny tight stretchy white top, blue gym shorts, and no shoes. She stepped up and looked down at me with an inscrutable expression.

"What?" I asked.

Kerrie put her legs astride mine, so now I was looking straight up at her. She stepped forward right up onto the couch so that she was now standing on the couch sticking her crotch right in my face, pushing my head against the wall. She grabbed my hair and held me there.

She said, "This is what you want, right?"

I nodded.

"Say it."

I mumbled into her pussy, "That's right. This is what I want."

Kerrie let go of my hair. "Damn right it is." She yanked down her gym shorts in front and shoved her pussy into my face. I eagerly went down on her and Kerrie began to moan and wiggle, standing on the couch, knocking my head back against the wall. Then she suddenly let go of the elastic waistband snapping up her shorts, turned, stepped off the couch, and walked right out of my apartment, leaving the door open.

Utterly dazed, I sat there with pure Kerrie smeared all over my face.

"Wow!"

The only possible drawback was the coconut oil that ended up all over my pillow and sheets, although I did kind of enjoy the memories the fragrance brought back after she'd leave. It made me think I was having an affair with a native girl on a Caribbean island.

I sat reading in the exact same spot on the couch. Kerrie came walking right into my apartment wearing a tight t-shirt with no bra, high-heeled sandals, and very tight red gym shorts that looked incredibly sexy on her. Without saying a word, she sauntered over to the window, leaned on the sill, and put her head outside to look around. I put the book down as Kerrie began shaking her gorgeous derriere at me. I sighed, put in the bookmark, set the book aside, stood up, stepped up behind her, took hold of her waist, and began rubbing myself against her ass. She rubbed back and began to moan, but didn't turn around. After a minute, I shrugged and pulled down her shorts revealing her lovely, chocolate brown ass. Kerrie didn't object or move, she just wiggled her bum. I grabbed hold of her waist and entered her from behind with her head still out the window. When I was about to come, I put both of my arms fully around her slim waist, grabbing her in a bear hug. As we collapsed forward there was a second when we both thought we might possibly fall out the window. Luckily, we didn't—we just fell to the floor. Kerrie reached behind her back, pushed me away, and pranced off into the bathroom.

I lay on the floor, rubbing my face and gasping for air.

"Oh, man."

A few days later I came up the stairs to find the door to apartment 7 wide open and the place completely empty. Kerrie had moved out without even telling me or saying goodbye or leaving a note or anything. Our relationship had lasted two erotic, sex-filled, coconut-scented months.

The sight of the empty apartment made me feel completely hollow inside.

"Bye," I mumbled, going back into to my tiny, empty little room and shutting the door.

> *OCTOBER 21, 1976*
> *I have just taken an hour-long shower. I'm exceedingly wrinkled and I'm having a hard time typing.*
> *Strangest thing happened during the shower . . .*
> *As I was soaping up the lights went out in the bathroom. I opened the shower curtain and the lights were out in the apartment also. I opened the window in the shower and stuck my head out and the whole corner was out. Traffic lights, streetlights, everything. About thirty seconds later everything went back on. However, not a single car went*

by during that whole thirty seconds.

Time stopped for thirty seconds on the corner of Melrose and Van Ness and I was the only one to see it.

Having quit Columbia College after one semester, I began the fall term at Los Angeles City College on Vermont Avenue and Melrose. LACC was supposed to have a very good acting and film department. I signed up for Screenwriting, Acting, and Cinematography. Luckily, they allowed prospective students to monitor the first class, and if you didn't like it you could drop it without being charged.

The screenwriting course was taught by the published science fiction author, Alan Dean Foster, who was marginally known for his novelizations of sci-fi movies, as well as the novelizations of the *Star Trek* cartoon series, although he'd never actually written a produced screenplay. When I first sat down in the class I noticed an interesting looking guy in the back row with long straight black hair, mirror shades, a white, button-up, short-sleeved shirt, black jeans, muscular chest and biceps, with his arms crossed and a skeptical expression on his face, tilting his chair back against the wall. Mr. Foster droned on and on for an hour and a half about the proper spacing of a screenplay, and where to set the tabs of your typewriter. He finally said, "Now go write a screenplay."

Outside after class, I lit a cigarette. The dude with the mirror shades stepped up. His voice was surprisingly low.

"Got an extra smoke?"

"Sure," I said, offering him a cigarette.

The guy took it and I gave him a light.

"Hi, I'm Josh Becker."

"Marvis."

I shook his very strong, calloused hand. "Good to meet you, Marv."

"It's Marvis, not Marv. Marvis is my last name."

"Oh. Sorry."

"What did you think of that class?" he asked.

"I wasn't very impressed. Telling us the tab stops, then saying 'Go write a screenplay' didn't seem very informative."

"No. It was bullshit. I'm not going back."

"Me, neither. I'm going to go check out Cinematography, how about you?"

Marvis said, "Yeah, me, too."

"So, you want to be a screenwriter?"

"Director," stated Marvis.

I nodded, "Me, too. And a screenwriter."

"What do you do?"

"To make a living, you mean?"

"Yeah."

"I'm a cashier at a deli. You?"

"I build film sets. I'm a carpenter."

"Cool."

Marvis shrugged. "It's okay, but I'd rather be a director."

"What are you working on now?"

"*Super Train.*"

"Oh," I said, "I've never seen it. That's that big dumb TV show, right?"

Marvis nodded, "Right. It's been a good gig, but it's been canceled."

We arrived at the classroom where Cinematography 101 was to be taught. Marvis and I took seats at the back.

Within just a few minutes, the white, male, middle-aged teacher stated categorically, "No one knows who cinematographers are. No one knows their names and never has. I assure you, nobody in this room could name 10 cinematographers under any circumstances."

Without a moment's hesitation my hand shot up into the air.

With a weary expression the teacher said, "Yes?"

I held up both of my closed fists, raising my fingers one by one to keep count: "Gordon Willis, John A. Alonzo, Conrad Hall, William Fraker, Gregg Toland, George Folsey, Joseph Ruttenberg, Vittorio Storaro, László Kovács, and Vilmos Zsigmond." I grinned widely. "How about 10 more?"

The teacher rolled his eyes in exasperation, stating, "That's not the point. The point is that *most* people don't know who cinematographers are . . ."

I stood up and walked out of the room. Marvis followed along right after me.

Once we were outside I said, "I've always wanted to do something like that. I mean, how often does someone ever make a statement like, 'Nobody here can name ten cinematographers'? Never."

Marvis asked, "You smoke pot?"

I said, "Whenever I can."

"You got a car?"

"Yeah."

"Follow me."

Marvis drove a military green 1958 Studebaker Commander station wagon, an easy car to keep an eye on in traffic since no other car looked anything like it. I followed him into downtown Hollywood, right near Hollywood High School and the Hotel Roosevelt, to Lanewood Avenue. Marvis lived in a huge old Hollywood mansion built in 1916, with a cracked cement birdbath on the front lawn, and a half dozen dismantled cars in the backyard. Also living there were four of his friends who were all from Cleveland, as was Marvis.

One of Marvis's friends living in the house was a pot dealer who presently had big bundles of Thai sticks. Marvis and I burned a big fat doob of Thai stick and got totally wasted—Thai-dyed. We began to excitedly tell each other science fiction stories that we'd read, and this went on for most of the night. We both kept notes on a pad on the table to remind ourselves of the stories we remembered while the other guy was talking.

Within a few hours we were best friends and we both knew it.

OCTOBER 23, 1976

Another day, however this has been a good one so far. Yesterday was good too. I talked with Marvis for hours yesterday and had a really good time. Marvis is incredibly smart in a very weird way. He seems to have a photographic memory, but no ambition at all. Although he says he wants to be director, I can tell he'll never even get close.

Today is very sunny and bright. The Hollywood sign is totally illuminated and visible for miles. Yesterday's rain washed away all the smog.

I woke up with a very pleasant feeling of déjà vu. It hasn't kept up, although it was nice while it lasted.

Why should I have to wait until I'm thirty before I can write long novels and full-length screenplays. I shouldn't.

DECEMBER 8, 1976

I just returned from the American Film Institute seminar with the great, old director, Rouben Mamoulian, which was very, very good.

Everyone at the seminar was a film student at AFI and they all asked real deep, esoteric, nonsensical questions that Mamoulian didn't know how to reply to.

AFI Student: What sort of film stock did you use?

Mamoulian: For the black & white films I used black & white stock, for the color films, I used color stock. Why?

He would just go into reminiscent monologues that were very interesting, but had nothing to do with the question.

As for myself, well, I asked some pretty good questions that elicited the best responses, if I do say so myself. Especially the question, "Who chose William Holden for Golden Boy?*"*

Rouben Mamoulian clasped his hands together, smiled and proudly replied, "Oh, I did. He was my greatest discovery."

Mamoulian's response to my last question, which was also the last question of the seminar, was the best though. I asked, "What did you think of Joseph Mankeiwicz's completed version of Cleopatra?*"*

Rouben Mamoulian stood, closed his eyes, shook his head in disgust and stated, "Oh my god, it was dreadful."

He got to exit on a big laugh, and I set him up.

In the middle of the night when I was in the shower I heard an exceptionally long tire screech and stuck my head out the open window in the shower just in time to see a silver Cadillac Seville skid right through the intersection, jump the curb, and crash right through the plate glass window of the Zodiac Café on the corner. Three-quarters of the car went into the restaurant before it stopped, with broken glass raining down all over the sidewalk. A moment later the front door of the restaurant opened and out stepped the furious drunk driver, a white, middle-aged guy in a suit and tie, with blood running down his face. He surveyed the damage and loudly proclaimed, *"Fuck!"*

I looked up and saw both Rex and Johnny with their heads out the window above me. They looked down, saw me, smiled, and waved. I waved back. I looked around and saw that heads were poking out of windows in many buildings, particularly over at the rat-hole Hollywood Executive Apartments.

I chuckled, "My community."

Not long after Kerrie moved out of apartment number 7, two guys right out of the navy, named Mark and Jim, moved in. Mark was a big, manly, muscular, redhead with a ruddy, freckled complexion. Jim was thin and pale, with a face full of pimples, and a slightly effeminate manner. They were apparently a couple. Mark didn't seem gay to me, but what did I know? The first time I met the two of them in the hallway, Mark looked around cautiously, then leaned forward and whispered in my ear, "You wanna buy some weed?"

I smiled widely. "Yes, I do."

As fate would have it, Mark and Jim turned out to be pot deal-ers. I couldn't believe my luck. Since Mark and Jim still had all of their customers in the navy, they would drive down to Camp Pendleton once a week and move as much dope as they could haul down there. Their supplier was in Florida, where Mark was from, and once a week they would receive a shoebox from Florida sent Federal Express that would contain a kilo of terrific shit. Pretty soon, though, they could move that entire kilo in a day or two in L.A. without ever supplying their main customers in the navy, and apparently their guy in Florida simply would not send any more than he was presently sending.

So Mark decided he would have to go to Florida himself and bring back as much pot as humanly possible so that he could make "the big score." How he would get there and back he didn't know since he wasn't about to take a very large quantity of pot on an airplane and he didn't have a car.

Meanwhile, I was still brokenhearted over Renée. I didn't have the money for long distance phone calls, but being a young writer I kept sending Renée long, typed love letters. To my chagrin, she wasn't writing back nearly as often as I was writing to her. Soon, she stopped writing back entirely.

I decided the hell with the cost, I'd just call her. I dialed the phone and miraculously she answered.

"Hello?"

"Renée? It's Josh."

"Oh, hi, Josh. What finally gets you to call?"

"I love you, that's what."

"Uh-huh."

"Uh-huh, what?"

"Uh-huh, that's good."

"Don't you love me?"

"I don't know. I think I do, then you go away and I don't know anymore."

"I want you to move out here with me."

"Josh, I'm in school at Eastern and doing really well. I'm not moving to L.A."

"You could go to UCLA."

"I don't want to go to UCLA. I like Eastern. Look, I'm going down to Miami with my family over the holidays. Is there any chance you could come down there?"

I was confused. "To Miami?" Did she somehow think that Miami was near Los Angeles?

"Uh-huh. We could hang out, get a tan, and talk about everything. Wouldn't that be great?"

I said, "Miami? That's a long way."

"Then don't go, what do I care?"

Renée hung up.

I just sat there with the dead phone in my hand.

"Miami?"

Postmarked Royal Oak, MI 24 Nov., 1976.
On blue flowered stationary.

> *Sun. 11-20*
> *9:40 P.M.*
> *Dear Josh,*
> *Well I just hung up the phone with you and I really don't have much to say. I don't remember the last time I've been this depressed. I wish you would have talked to me. I need to hear your voice. I know I'm not making sense. I just have to be relating to you somehow and since I can't speak to you on the phone I guess that's why I'm writing*

a letter. Oh fuck. I'm not making sense. All I know is I need you so badly I feel so helpless I can't have you. I wish either you stayed or that I didn't see you. I can't go on like this. It's not fair. I want you. I'm so upset I'm not making sense. This letter is ridiculous. I probably won't even send it but if you're reading it I guess I did. Shit what am I saying what am I writing.

I guess it all amounts to 3 words, I love you.
Renee

I looked up from the letter. "She loves me."

Then it all fell into place—Mark and I would drive my car down to Miami. Mark would pay the expenses and score weed, and I would see Renée. Once Renée and I were face to face again there was no doubt in my mind that it would all work out, just like in the movies. We both loved each other, and that's all that mattered, right?

I suggested the plan to Mark and he immediately accepted—he'd happily pay all the expenses both coming and going.

It was written in the stars.

So, in late December, 1976, Mark and I set off for Florida in my yellow rotary wagon. Los Angeles to Miami is a *very* long drive—3,000 miles, maybe a bit more— with 1,000 miles of it across the widest section of Texas. The directions could not be easier: get on Interstate-10, which begins at the beach in L.A., go east for 2,500 miles until you reach Florida, then make a right turn heading south on I-75 for 500 more miles.

To aid in the long drive, Mark had scored an ounce of weed, three grams of cocaine, and a baggy full of pharmaceutical speed: Dexies, Bennies, Christmas Trees, and Black Beauties. The idea was to drive straight through without stopping at hotels to sleep, thus saving money.

Mark had also thoughtfully brought along a white china dinner plate so that the passenger could cut lines of coke, hand the plate and a rolled up $100 bill to the driver, then take the steering wheel while the driver snorted the lines. Luckily, there wasn't a bend in the road all the way through California, New Mexico, Arizona, and Texas—about 2,000 miles—so we never worried at all about getting too fucked-up to drive.

I had an eight-track player in my car, but most of my eight-track tapes were broken, and since it seemed like a dying technology, I'd stopped buying them. My only functioning eight-track tapes were: *Dark Side of the Moon* and *Meddle* by Pink Floyd, *Hank Williams' Greatest Hits*, and *Working Man's Dead* by the Grateful Dead, which I didn't like and wasn't even sure how I'd gotten. So we ended up listening to the radio most of the way. Inexplicably, the big hit for the previous month had been "Tonight's the Night" by Rod Stewart, a run-of-the-mill song if there ever was one, and it was on every channel all the time. Also playing excessively were such truly horrible songs as "Muskrat Love" by Captain & Tennille, "You Make Me Feel Like Dancing" by Leo Sayer, "More Than a Feeling" by Boston, "The Rubberband Man" by the Spinners, and the particularly awful novelty hit, "Disco Duck" by Rick Dees. A good big hit song that was on a lot was "Night Moves" by Bob Seger, but it always reminded me of Detroit and made me feel homesick. There was also "Sorry Seems to be the Hardest Word" by Elton John, but that always reminded me of Renée and made me feel sad.

In the middle of the night, in the long, lonely stretch of I-10 between El Paso and San Antonio, Mark had his eyes closed but was definitely awake while I drove and searched up and down the radio dial for a station. After running slowly all the way up and down the dial several times, suddenly there was the Electric Light Orchestra singing "Livin' Thing" and coming in crystal clear. I thought, "Okay, that's a pretty good song," and left it.

When the song ended the DJ came on. "That was ELO with 'Livin' Thing,' number 16 on the top 20, up from number 18 last week. This is CKLW-Windsor, Ontario."

I couldn't believe it. I said, "Windsor? That's right across from Detroit. That's gotta be over a thousand miles from here."

Mark nodded and grunted, "Big fuckin' deal."

I waved my hand in disgust. Mark didn't understand and never could. You had to be from Detroit for this to matter. Or Windsor, of course.

CKLW magically held for over an hour, playin' all the hits, then slowly faded away as we neared San Antonio and began picking up the local radio stations. I was a little sad when CKLW finally faded away completely.

Once we finally got across Texas, the scenery thankfully became quite cool going through Baton Rouge, New Orleans, and Mobile, with a lot of bridges, wetlands, and moss-covered trees. When we arrived in New Orleans at 5:30 A.M., completely, utterly, and totally wired on cocaine, speed, and pot, we stopped at McDonald's to get breakfast. We both ordered Egg McMuffins and coffee, sat down near the window, and watched the day begin in the French Quarter of New Orleans. No sidewalks, with old buildings abutting the street, decorated with black wrought-iron grille-work.

Suddenly, it seemed like everyone was leaving the McDonald's at the same time in a hurry, including all the employees.

Mark and I were so stoned and caught up in our own heads that we didn't find anything out of the ordinary in this.

The last McDonald's employee out the door, a young black man, turned and said to us, "You two better get outta here 'cause the whole fuckin' kitchen's on fire."

Mark and I turned around to see that the kitchen was completely engulfed in flames. Grinning stupidly, we both looked at each other and exclaimed, "*Whoa!*" Hastily, we grabbed the remainder of our breakfasts and stumbled outside with everybody else, just as two fire engines arrived.

As flames consumed the whole building, Mark and I and a crowd on the street all watched the firemen battle the blaze. Soon, however, we grew bored. As the sun began to rise on a clear sunny day in New Orleans, Mark and I dazedly wandered the streets of the French Quarter.

Oddly, at 6:00 A.M. all the bars were open. We went into a cool dark place and had a beer. We were both seriously grinding our teeth and chain-smoking cigarettes.

Mark loudly blurted out, "I'm not gay, you know."

I looked around to see if anyone else had heard, but the place was empty. "You're not? What does Jim think about that?"

"He's gay. I'm *bi*."

"Okay."

"I just didn't want you thinkin' I was gay is all."

"Okay."

"I like girls, and I've fucked a whole lot of 'em."

"Okay."

"You'll see. I've got a ton a girlfriends in Florida."

"Cool."

"Maybe you and your girlfriend, and me and one of my girl-friends will double-date one night."

I nodded. "Sounds great. You'll like Renée. She's terrific. And gorgeous, too."

Mark pointed in my face and stated loudly, "I've fucked *plenty* of gorgeous women."

There was no one in the place, but still. I said, "That's great. Just keep your hands off Renée."

"I don't need *your* girlfriend. I've got my *own* girlfriends, comin' out my ears."

"Okay then."

"I just did what I had to do while I was in the navy, under-stand?"

"Sure," I said, not understanding, but not wanting to start trou-ble.

"Okay, then. Let's get the fuck outta this town."

We got back on the road and kept driving.

As Mark drove, I sat there in the passenger seat looking at him and thinking, "I've been horny in my life plenty, but never horny enough to, A, become gay, or B, fuck anything as pimply and ugly as Jim, in the ass no less. Jesus-fuckin'-Christ!" I shuddered. Mark glanced at me and I became totally paranoid. "Oh, fuck! He knows what I'm thinking." I nervously lit my 7,000th cigarette in the past 24 hours and sincerely thought, "Oh, yeah, *this* is the good one." I blew smoke rings at the dashboard, watching them hit, expand, and disperse with great amusement, even if my jaw was clicking and hurt.

After what seemed like a million more miles, we finally arrived at Mark's mother's house in the outskirts of Ft. Lauderdale (I never heard a word about where his father was). The house was located in a bleak suburb full of small, square, aging homes with fake-wood vinyl siding. Mark's mother was a pleasant, petite woman in her mid-40s who didn't seem to give a shit about anything except keeping her house clean. In the living room there was thick brown shag carpeting, a big old organ with a lot of switches, and a nearly life-size painting of Jesus on the wall.

I called Renée's parents' condo in Miami a few times and it just rang and rang. What the hell?

Meanwhile, Mark needed my car to go make his dope deals and didn't want me along, so I ended up sitting in the living room with Mark's mom. Both of us read books, drank coffee, and smoked cigarettes all day long. She read a gothic romance and I read *Tai-Pan* by James Clavell, which, luckily for me, was both a terrific book and very long.

Every hour or so I would call Renée's number again, and it would ring and ring and no one would answer. I'd sit back down on the couch, a little bit more depressed each time.

Mark's mom looked sympathetic. "It'll be all right, dear. How about another cup of coffee?"

"Sure, thanks."

She went to the kitchen for more coffee, saying, "I'm sure she's just out with her family somewhere."

"No doubt."

"She'll call."

Mark's mom returned with two more cups of coffee, set them on coasters on the table, and sat back down. After a long moment she asked . . .

"What kind of friends are Mark and Jim?"

I smiled. "Good friends."

"How good?"

"They're navy buddies."

"Hmmm." She looked like she might say something else, but didn't.

We both lit cigarettes, picked up our books, and kept reading.

This was handwritten in red ink in a stenographer's pad, with the spiral binding at the top.

DECEMBER 23, 1976

I have been fucked! I have driven 3,000 miles, from L.A. to Miami Beach for one single solitary reason, to see Renee, and she will not see me.

She says that she has "obligations" but all they really are are things that she always does in Florida and has grown used to doing while she's here. My presence is not usual and therefore cannot be worked in.

    I really don't think she sees just how much she's hurting me. Or she doesn't care.

    However, if she does not repent her sins and evil doings by tomorrow I will be so mad . . . So mad . . .

    I don't really know what I'll do.

That night, I was camped out on a cot in Mark's bedroom and Mark was in his bed. Just as I was teetering on the edge of sleep, there was a knock on the window. A cute, wild-haired blonde girl of about 20 stood there holding up a bottle of booze, grinning, and clearly falling-down drunk.

Mark turned to me. "You see. I told you so."

Mark opened the window and helped the cute chick climb in, and she was totally wasted.

She proclaimed, "Mark, you're back!"

Mark said, "Shhh," then turned to me. "Hey, man, could you go to the living room?"

I said, "Sure. No problem." I got up from the cot, took the blanket, the pillow, my cigarettes and lighter, and *Tai-Pan*, and left the room. The door locked after me.

I sat in the living room reading and smoking, listening to Mark and the cute drunk chick noisily fuck their brains out.

I said to myself, "I guess he's not gay. He's bi."

In the stenographer's pad in red ink.

    DECEMBER 24, 1976

    It is 1:00 PM and I am sitting in Mark's bedroom in his mother's house in Sunrise, FL just outside Ft. Lauderdale without a single fucking reason for being here.

    I just got off the phone with Renee and her coldness is more than I can take. She really doesn't care whether we see each other or not. She truly doesn't care.

    As we talked on the phone I could do nothing else but cry. Either she didn't hear or it simply means nothing to her because her frigid coldness persisted throughout.

    Not only does Renee not love me, but she doesn't even care how I feel. I mean nothing to her.

I'd have to say that it is over, with me being the hurt party once again.

Mark and I stayed in Florida for a couple of days as Mark made a variety of different dope deals—three kilos from this guy, four kilos from that guy, three more from this other guy. He brought me along on one of the transactions. We drove to an even bleaker, though newer, suburb where the houses looked like pre-fabricated boxes on an utterly barren, flat landscape. We entered a small house with an inordinately large, ridiculously ornate Christmas tree that seemed to take up a quarter of the whole house. Mark and a friendly Latino guy went off into the back to do the deal, leaving me in the festive living room with a pile of cocaine on a mirror the size of a baseball and a casual "Help yourself" as they left. I snorted several big fat lines of coke, then Mark and the dealer returned. Mark was holding a full black garbage bag containing six kilos of gorgeous blonde Columbian pot. I purchased one pound of this stuff from Mark, at wholesale for $200.

Renée finally called me back at 8:00 A.M. the next morning, waking up everyone in the house. I took the phone from Mark's mom, who whispered, "See, I told you so."

"Good morning, Renée."

Renée sounded distressed. "Look, Josh, could you meet me in the parking lot in a few minutes?"

"A few minutes? No. It's about 20 miles, I think."

Renée sighed in exasperation. "Okay, how about an hour?"

"Okay. How do I get there?"

"I don't know. Here's the address."

Renée gave me the address in Miami Beach and hung up.

Mark's mom explained how to get there, then I got dressed in a hurry and took off. I drove south on the I-95 freeway for a long way, got off in an area that was nothing but identical high-rise apartment buildings, and amazingly was just pulling into the parking lot of Renée's parents' condo at the stroke of an hour.

The high-rise condo's parking lot looked just like a Cadillac sales lot—there were hundreds of Cadillacs of every color and model, as well as a few Mercedes and Lincolns tossed in for variety. I sat there in my Mazda and smoked a cigarette.

"I drive 25 miles and I'm on time. She has to come down a goddamn elevator and she's late."

Renée finally came out the front door. She was just in jeans and a t-shirt, and she looked terrific. She peered around, spotted my completely unique yellow wagon, waved her hand, then slowly came walking up. She opened the passenger door and got in.

Renée looked at me and asked, "Josh, what are you doing down here?"

"You suggested it. It was *your* idea."

"But I had no idea you'd take me seriously, and *drive* here, no less."

"Well I did."

"Why?"

"Why? Because I love you, that's why."

Renée turned away from me and stared out the side window. "Look, I'm not moving to L.A. and you won't move back to Michigan, so there it is."

"Why won't you move to L.A.?"

She turned and looked at me. "Because I don't want to, okay? Why don't you move back home?"

"I just moved to L.A."

Renée looked back out the window, "Fine."

"Don't you love me?"

"I don't know. Maybe I don't."

I felt like I'd been hit in the gut with a telephone pole. "Oh."

Renée quickly reached out and touched my hand. "I mean, I do love you, Josh, just not enough to move to L.A. Look, I gotta go."

I was horrified. "But you just got here. I just got here."

"My family's waiting for me. Bye."

She kissed me on the cheek, got out of the car, and quickly walked away across the expansive parking lot. As I sat there in my little yellow wagon watching Renée walk out of my life, possibly forever, all I could think was, "Man, what a great ass."

Mark and I now had to drive the 3,000 miles back home, but on this leg of the journey we had three large cardboard boxes in the back of the wagon loaded with 16 kilos of marijuana. Mark had also scored an ounce of cocaine for good measure. We still had most of the speed left, as well. So we decided that we wouldn't stop to sleep on the way back, either—we'd just drive straight on through like the last time.

As we drove we conducted a running comparative taste-test between the many different kinds of pot we had on board. It was all good. We were also trying our damnedest to snort the entire ounce of coke. An ounce is *a lot of cocaine*! Mark and I snorted cocaine nonstop for the next 1,500 miles. The only time we stopped snorting coke was to try smoking a different kind of pot. As we did this we drove through the bayou country where the highway was suspended on cement pylons over miles of dark brackish water with nothing but dead sticks poking out, undoubtedly teeming with alligators and snakes, and seemingly a bad place to get too high and drive off the road. We drove back through New Orleans without stopping, then back into the endless expanse of Texas—absolutely dead-ass flat terrain for a thousand miles, with nothing but the occasional butte lurking in the distance.

Meanwhile, cocaine is a drug of diminishing returns. The first few lines are great, the next few lines are pretty great, the next few lines after that are okay, down the scale until you reach the stage where you basically feel like hammered shit with your teeth welded shut, snorting more and more coke in a desperate, though futile, attempt to get back that first great buzz.

Halfway through Texas we could not sit in the car anymore—we were both ready to spontaneously combust. When we got to Kerrville, west of San Antonio, we knew we had to stop, although there was no question that there'd be no sleeping—we'd Hoovered up three or four grams of cocaine each over the previous 50 hours of nonstop driving, as well as an endless supply of weed, and let's not forget those terrific little Black Beauties.

We got a hotel room in Kerrville. The first thing Mark did was to take the 5-foot-tall, full-length mirror off the wall, lay it on the bed, then proceeded to cut two lines of cocaine, five feet long each. Snorting a 5-foot-long line of coke may seem like a physical impossibility, but it's not, particularly with good coke, which this was.

On our way into town we'd passed a big disco, and decided that once we were sufficiently coked up again, we'd go check it out.

After performing this incredible feat of narcotic nasal inhalation, we then dressed up in our fancy duds. Christmas 1976 was the beginning of the disco craze, with bell bottoms, unbuttoned Roland polyester shirts, ridiculously tall platform shoes, and big hair on both the girls and the boys.

As Mark primped in the bathroom mirror with a blow-dryer, he said, "We're gonna disco these Texas babes like they've never been discoed before! Right in front of their sorry, lame-ass, cowboy-hat-wearin', motherfuckin' boyfriends!"

I nodded, "Fuck yeah!"

"We're gonna walk into that place like we fucking own it! We've had more cocaine than everybody in this whole fucking town put together!"

"Goddamn right we have!"

"Maybe in all of Texas!"

"Yeah we have!"

"And then we're gonna bring a couple those Texas bitches back here, and fuck their brains out!"

"Okay!"

"Let's move it out!"

"Yes, sir!"

Mark and I walked into that Texas disco like we fuckin' owned the place—except that it was damn near empty. There were six or seven couples spread out around a roller rink-sized building, lit in red and blue with a revolving disco-ball over the dance floor, which was presently unused. Donna Summer sang "Love to Love You Baby" at an ungodly decibel level.

Mark and I looked around and shrugged. Mark snorted, rubbing his red nose, "Figures. Let's drink some beer."

We then proceeded to drink as many pitchers of beer as we possibly could in the hour before closing time, in an utterly useless attempt to calm down a little bit.

Closing the place at 2:00 A.M., Mark and I went back to the hotel room, snorted a lot more coke off the long mirror, took showers, and split.

When we arrived back in Los Angeles, 50 or so hours later, we were both a serious mess. We were so wired that we could no longer speak, our jaws were welded shut, and had been all the way since Albuquerque. But we'd made it, with the shit—over 35 pounds of good weed. When L.A. was dry.

I took my pound and put it in the fridge. I then climbed into the shower, turned the hot water up as far as I could stand it, and stayed there for two hours, until I was so wrinkly I was forced to get out. Lying naked on the bed smoking a cigarette, my hands were shaking so much that I could barely get the cigarette to my mouth.

Through gritted teeth I hissed, "This too shall pass."

Leigh's letter was waiting for me. It was written on lined spiral notebook paper with shredded holes.

> Postmarked Dearborn, MI, 16 December, 1976
>
> *Dearest Joshua:*
>
> *It's been a long time. I've fallen into severe misfortune, become suicidal and have had to be hospitalized. I hope to be better soon but I don't know whether I can ever trust myself again. The pressure of returning to U of M and mostly of living in an apartment by myself proved to [sic] much for me and I had a breakdown. I would appreciate any letters you could send me to cheer me up. I spoke briefly with your mother to get your address, you sound as if you're doing well. I wish you all the success in the world. Has anything big happened? Do you have a girlfriend yet? Right now I would be her if I could. Please write and tell me all that Rona Barrett doesn't,*
>
> *Love,*
> *Leigh*

I read the letter again and again, but each time I still didn't know what to say. I set Leigh's letter on my desk beside my typewriter, telling myself I'd answer it later. It sat there for days. Each time I saw the letter I made some feeble attempt at composing a response to Leigh in my head, then quickly gave up. Finally, after about a week, I folded Leigh's letter up, slid it back in the envelope, and hid it in the bottom drawer.

I never wrote back.

Also waiting for me upon my return from Florida were Chanukah checks from my parents for $50, my grandma and grandpa on my dad's side for $25, and from my grandma, my mom's mom, for $25 more, equaling a whopping $100.

I thought, "Now, what can I do with this?"

Opening the door to Nagoya Massage, I entered the small lobby and asked the older Asian woman at the desk, "Is Alice here?"

"Sure, you go in. Room three."

She buzzed me in.

I walked down the hall, stopped at room 3 and went in. I was giddy. Just how much "more" was available, and at what price?

Cute little Alice with the bangs walked in, immediately recognized me, and smiled. "You come back. You had coupon, right?"

"Yeah," I said. "That was me."

"You have another coupon?"

"No."

"Where you been? That was a long time ago."

"Oh, you know . . ." I shrugged.

"You take off all your clothes, I come right back, okay?"

"Okay."

When Alice returned some inordinate amount of time later, I had stripped naked and had a towel over my eager hard-on. Alice pointed and smiled.

"You already hard. That good. Save me lots of trouble. You want the same as before?"

"Um . . . last time I was here, you said, 'with more money you can get more.' I was wondering what you meant by that exactly?"

Alice nodded. "Twenty-five standard massage. Fifty blow-job. One hundred everything."

Grinning, I said, "Everything."

Alice smiled back. "You get Christmas check from home?"

"Yeah, as a matter of fact, I did," I laughed.

"This the right place to spend it, too. Okay, everything. You lie down."

I lay back down on the massage table, keeping the towel over my lap. Alice went over to a drawer below the stack of towels and took out a foil-wrapped condom. She waved it at me, raising her eyebrows. Putting the condom between her teeth, Alice untied her robe, letting it fall open. I could just catch a glimpse of her pussy as she slowly walked forward. She then pushed the robe off her shoulders and let it drop to the floor. Her body was perfect —as perfect as a slim, trim, small-breasted, 20-year-old Asian girl could possibly be. There wasn't an extra pinch of skin anywhere. Her pubic hair was black and trimmed in a thin vertical strip.

I stopped breathing.

Alice slowly tore open the condom package, tossed the wrapper over her shoulder, then stepped up to me. She removed the towel from my lap and set it aside. My woody was sticking straight up and vibrating like a high-tension electrical cable. Alice opened her mouth and put the condom in. She took hold of me in both of her small hands, then put the condom on me by use of her mouth. Alice used her fingers to roll the condom all the way down while she kept sucking on my now latex-sheathed dick.

Luckily for me, the condom decreased the sensation so that I was able to hold onto himself. Just. I was actually able to relax a little bit, too. So I reached out and took hold of her firm little ass. Maneuvering my hand around and up, the ends of my fingers just found their way up into the warmth between her legs.

After a few more minutes, Alice stopped sucking, stood up straight, but kept a firm grip on me. She put one knee on the cushioned table, swung her other leg over my legs while holding onto me for leverage. Alice now took me in both hands, looked down into my eyes, smiled ever so slightly, raising her eyebrows up to her bangs.

I gripped the sides of the massage table. Alice raised her whole body up, got on top of me, then ever so slowly eased herself down. Were it not for the condom, I would have most certainly come. She placed her open palms on my chest and began to go gently up and down, sighing contentedly as she moved. I began to sigh in unison, reaching up and cupping her little breasts, circling my thumbs around on her nipples. Alice closed her eyes and opened her mouth. I kept my eyes open so I wouldn't miss a second of this—I wanted it burned into my memory forever, for future reference.

After a few minutes of this, Alice opened her eyes and asked, "You wanna change positions?"

I nodded, "Sure. I'll get on top."

"Okay."

We switched positions.

Once on top I began banging her as hard as I could.

Alice whispered in my ear, "Shhhh, you slow down, okay? No hurry."

I said, "Okay," and slowed way down.

"Much better."

I closed my eyes and went at it slowly for a short while. Then I opened my eyes and looked down at this gorgeous little Asian doll beneath me, sighing happily, holding onto my shoulders, and that was it. Gasping, I just came and came. I finally collapsed on top of her while shaking all over. She stroked my hair.

"Oooh, yeah, it so good. You go, baby. Go ahead."

As soon as I stopped quivering, Alice got out from beneath me, found a box of tissues, and pulled out four. She quickly grabbed hold of me with the tissues and removed the used condom. She threw out the tissues and condom, then grabbed three more tissues and wiped me off.

"All good now."

I sighed, "Yeah, it is."

She threw out the tissues and put on her robe. "You good boy. We have very good fun. You come back. We do that again, okay?"

"Sure. Next Christmas."

"No. Before that."

"I'll do my best," I shrugged.

"You get dressed."

I put on my underwear and my jeans, took my wallet out of my pocket, counted out the money, and handed her five twenties and a ten, completely cleaning me out. Alice smiled.

"You come back, okay? Ask for Alice."

"I will."

Alice opened the door for me, and as I went by she gave my ass a pat. Good job.Out on the boulevard in the cool night air, I lit a smoke.

"Wow! That was the best Christmas present I ever got. Gotta make sure to thank the grandparents."

Having made their big score, Mark and Jim promptly moved out of 666 North Van Ness, #7. They left in the middle of the night and didn't say goodbye. When I came out in the morning I saw that apartment 7 was empty again, with the door wide open. I felt like I was kicked in the stomach, again. I thought we were friends.

I turned around and found a piece of lined paper taped to my door. I took it down, unfolded it, and found that it was a pretty good ballpoint pen drawing by Jim of a man sitting at the kitchen table looking at a newspaper, with the caption, "Every day the paperboy brings more."

"Huh, I suppose I do play Pink Floyd kind of a lot."

I went back into my apartment, put on *Dark Side of the Moon*, closed the door, then smoked a joint out of my own personal pound.

A few months later, I was talking on the phone to my old friend Jim from high school who said, "Oh, did you hear about Leigh Albertson?"

"No, what?"

"She committed suicide."

I was mortified. "What? How?"

"I don't know. But she'd been in and out of the hospital a bunch of times in the past few years, and she kept having nervous breakdowns. Wasn't she your girlfriend for a while in junior high?"

I nodded and sighed. "Yeah, she was." I was about to add that a few months ago she'd stayed with me for a couple of days, but I just couldn't bring myself to go into it.

I glanced down at the bottom drawer, thinking, "Maybe, if I'd only answered her letter, she wouldn't have killed herself."

Having decided not to take any classes at LACC, but still trying to satisfy my parents' demand that I stay in school, I signed up at Sherwood Oaks Experimental College on Hollywood Boulevard and Ivar, located above a shoe store. It was experimental to the extent that there were no tests, no essays, no required work at all. The school brought in top professional filmmakers for question and answer sessions, and whatever you got out of that was up to you. Apparently, Rod Serling had something to do with the school's inception, and they had a scholarship named for him, as well as a big painting of him in stark silhouette on one wall.

I attended Q&A sessions with Robert Aldrich, Mel Brooks, Robert DeNiro, Martin Scorsese, François Truffaut, Gene Wilder, and Robert Wise, among others.

Just knowing that most people didn't realize that Mel Brooks had won an Oscar in 1968 for his screenplay of *The Producers*, I asked him, "Where do you keep your Oscar?"

Brooks smiled happily. "Most people don't know that I won an Oscar, for Best Original Screenplay for *The Producers*, and I keep it on top of my mother's TV set in Miami. My wife keeps hers on top of her mother's TV set in Brooklyn."

Since this question went over so well, when Robert DeNiro spoke at the Writer's Guild Theater the next week, I asked the same question, "Where do you keep your Oscar?"

DeNiro looked at me suspiciously, as though he thought I intended to steal his Oscar. "In my apartment. Why?"

"No reason," I mumbled, sliding down into my seat trying to disappear.

A woman seated in front of me said loudly, "What a stupid question."

When they interrupted the interview to show some clips from DeNiro's films, all of which I had already seen, I ducked out into the empty lobby for a cigarette. I lit up, and a moment later the door to the auditorium opened and out stepped Robert DeNiro. Now it was just me and DeNiro standing there in the lobby.

I said, "I'm the guy who asked the stupid question about your Oscar." DeNiro nodded. I continued on, "You see, I asked Mel Brooks that same question last week, and it went over very well, probably because no one knew he'd won an Oscar. Whereas you just won yours two years ago so everybody knows you've got one. See?"

The interviewer stuck his head out the door and said, "We're back on."

Robert DeNiro smiled, turned and went back in, having not said a word.

I felt like a complete asshole.

"I guess that explains it then."

I went back in for the rest of the interview, but DeNiro wasn't in a very talkative mood. When asked, "What do you think of the violence in your movies?"

DeNiro replied, "I don't think about it." Otherwise it was all yes and no answers.

After the interview, I was the first one out of the theater. I got outside the glass doors in to the vestibule and lit a smoke. I watched through the glass as the audience of a couple hundred people filled the lobby. A moment later Robert DeNiro and the actress, Dianne Abbott, stepped into the lobby and attempted to make their way through the crowd, but the people started to push in tighter. WGA Theater employees tried to clear a path, but too many people were all jammed in together too tightly. It was a creepy, miniature version of *The Day of the Locust*. Eventually, Robert DeNiro and Dianne Abbott got through the crowd and out the glass doors to the vestibule. Now it was just the two of them and me. They both shook their heads, blinking and sighing as though they'd just been through an ordeal, which they had.

Robert DeNiro looked up and saw me standing there all by myself leaning up against the wall smoking a cigarette. DeNiro smiled, pointed at me and said, "See ya." Then he and Ms. Abbott split.

I grinned. I wasn't one of *them*, the locusts, even if I did ask stupid questions.

Just a few minutes later, the great director Robert Wise (Oscars for *West Side Story* and *The Sound of Music*) pulled up in a gold Jaguar. Who should he happen upon standing there smoking a cigarette but me.

Robert Wise asked me, "Do you know where I can park?"

I asked in a wry tone, "Is that a Volkswagen?"

Robert Wise replied dryly, "No, it's a Jaguar," and drove away.

I felt like a total idiot. "Boy oh boy, I'm knockin' 'em dead today."

My first question for Robert Wise was, "What was it like editing *Citizen Kane*?" and this brought on a 10-minute, supremely interesting answer about working with Orson Welles. I felt proud to have asked such a good question that had inspired such a lengthy response.

My next question was, "Whose idea was it to have the Saul Bass graphic of Manhattan changing colors at the beginning of *West Side Story*?"

Wise said, "Mine," then pointed at someone else and said, "Yes?"

I thought, "Huh, that didn't work quite as well as the first one."

After considerable reflection, I then asked, "What did you think of the *Night Gallery* remake of your film, *The Body Snatcher*?"

Robert Wise looked shocked. "I didn't know they'd remade it. Who was in it?"

"Cornel Wilde," I said. "It wasn't bad, but it wasn't as good as the original."

Wise said, "Thank you. Yes, that was a good picture. Val Lewton produced it . . ." and he was off and running on a long, interesting answer about working at RKO in the '40s.

I felt vindicated for calling Wise's Jaguar a VW.

On another night François Truffaut was interviewed, with an interpreter. Actually, he understood the questions, but he answered in French, then was translated, making the whole process a drag. But first they showed his film *Day for Night*, a film that seemingly *everybody* loved, had gotten stellar reviews, was nominated for several Oscars, including Best Director, and I just flat-out didn't like it. All of these dull French film crew members diddling each other, while they unbelievably made an utterly insipid-looking movie.

As I thought about it during Truffaut's dull Q&A, which all died going back and forth through the translator, I really didn't like *any* of Truffaut's movies and I'd actually seen a lot of them. I did sort of like his first film, *The 400 Blows*, although I wasn't really in love with it, either.

Then, for some unbeknownst reason, after the interview I found myself in line to speak to François Truffaut. When I got up to him I said to the translator, as sincerely as I could considering that I was completely insincere, "Please tell him I've enjoyed *all* of his movies."

Truffaut obviously understood without translation and replied, just as insincerely, "*Merci beaucoup,*" shook my hand, and moved me along.

Next.

Before Robert Aldrich spoke to the class we screened his newest film, *Twilight's Last Gleaming*. Even though I admired Aldrich, and really liked many of my films, like *Vera Cruz, Apache, Attack, Whatever Happened to Baby Jane?, The Dirty Dozen, The Flight of the Phoenix,* and *The Longest Yard,* I just hated *Twilight's Last Gleaming,* with all of its stupid, pointless split-screen, and it just went on and on for 146 miserable minutes, so that now I was in a bad mood and had a headache. I looked down at the Xeroxed handout listing all of Robert Aldrich's films in chronological order, and suddenly my hand shot up, as though of its own accord. Aldrich pointed at me.

"Yes?"

I spoke in the tone of a prosecuting attorney, "Why have all of your films since 1960 been longer than two hours? Is two hours now insufficient to tell a story? I might add that *Citizen Kane* is only 119 minutes."

Robert Aldrich rather innocently replied, "I didn't realize they were."

"They are," I stated flatly.

"Huh."

"Why is that?"

"I don't know."

But I wasn't done. "All right. What was the point of all the split-screen in this film?"

Robert Aldrich said, "I had a lot of good footage and I wanted to use it all."

I rolled my eyes, thinking, "Good god, what a stupid reason for using split-screen."

As I walked home that night along Hollywood Boulevard I wondered at myself, "How could I have picked on Robert Aldrich like that? He's an old man and he made some of my favorite movies. I'm such an asshole!"

One night when I returned home from helping a classmate at Sherwood Oaks edit a Super 8 movie, I came trotting up the front steps of the building holding my little Super 8 viewer and editing supplies to find a small party going on in apartment 1, which was used for storage. There was Dan in his cowboy hat, Rex in his kimono, an old man in a robe from the first floor whom I did not know, and a thin, lanky Mexican handyman who had apparently been helping Dan that day. They were all lounging on old furniture and drinking whiskey from paper cups.

Dan said, "Hey, Josh, come on in. Have a drink."

I stepped into the apartment. "What are you drinking?"

Dan held up a half gallon of Jim Beam. "Whiskey."

I don't like whiskey, but I decided to be friendly. "Sure. Thanks."

Wending my way through all the knees and junky furniture, I sat down on a milk crate against the back wall.

Dan poured a paper cup full of whiskey and handed it to me. I took it trying not to spill. The smell was vile.

Dan lifted his cup. "*Skol.*"

We all drank. I took a small sip and winced. *Blech!*

After a perfectly pleasant five minutes, all at once the Mexican man seemed to have very suddenly had too much to drink. He rose unsteadily to his feet and pointed down at Dan.

"*You fucking asshole!*" he drunkenly slurred with a Mexican accent.

Dan couldn't believe it. "*What?*"

The Mexican man stepped up closer to Dan, swaying over him, pointing in his face. "You heard me, you fuckin' asshole." He pointed at everyone else in the room. "*Piece of shit motherfuckers!*"

Dan immediately stood up and left the room. The Mexican man then turned on Rex.

"You fucking faggot!"

Rex darted right out of the room like a ballet dancer. A second later the old man in the robe left, too. All of them had been near the door, whereas I was against the back wall and now had the drunk Mexican *between* myself and the door. I sat there on the milk crate holding the little paper cup of smelly whiskey and smiling lamely. The Mexican man turned back into the room, saw there was no one left but me, drunkenly staggered up to me, and stood over me pointing down in my face and yelling, "*Fucking faggot!*"

I sat there with a pained smile watching this guy drunkenly looming over me, screaming and swaying like he was on the deck of a rolling ship. Then out of nowhere the son of a bitch hauled off and slugged me as hard as he could with a solid right hook to my temple—with a big ring on his finger. There was a momentary flash of a single yellow star on a black background, followed by an enormous rush of pain. As I slowly opened my eyes I found the Mexican man still standing over me, his fists clenched and raised, seemingly ready to punch me again. Instinctively, I lifted my foot and kicked him in the gut with all of my strength. He flew backward across the room, landing on a couch. I stood to leave and now I was also swaying like I was on a ship due to the punch to the temple. I touched the bruise, looked at my hand and it was bloody.

"Holy shit!"

I picked up my little Super 8 viewer, walked past the Mexican man lying on the couch who was holding his belly, and exited apartment number 1. As I entered the foyer the Mexican man jumped on my back from behind causing us both to crash down on the stinky red carpet. Every tenant in the building had crowded into the lobby to see the fight. The drunk Mexican sat up on my back and began slugging me in the back of the head.

Having been a decent wrestler in high school, I easily twisted out from beneath the guy. As we both got to our feet I threw one straight jab directly into the guy's belly, immediately doubling him over. I then easily grabbed him in a headlock, my absolute favorite fight maneuver—once you've got someone in a headlock, for all intents and purposes they've lost the fight since there's no way to get out of it and you can cut off their breathing at will, which has a serious impact on their decision-making abilities. The Mexican man tried to hit me a few more times in the back, but each time he tried I'd just tighten my grip on his throat cutting off his breathing, so he quickly quit. He tried to punch me again, so I cut off his breathing again. After a few minutes of this routine, I suddenly just let go, pushing him hard away from me. I then jumped to my feet, stepping as far away from the guy as possible. The Mexican man just lay there on his face. After a moment he began to puke all over the red carpeting.

That's just about when the LAPD arrived. Dan had called them as soon as he'd left apartment number 1.

The two uniformed cops casually watched the Mexican man retch, lying there heaving in his own vomit, then looked up and asked, "What happened?"

Dan and Rex both animatedly told the story. I just stood there smoking a cigarette, occasionally touching the swelling bruise beside my left eye. At least it stopped bleeding.

The cops asked me, "You okay?"

I said, "Yeah, I'm fine."

"You wanna press charges?"

I shook my aching head. "No."

The cops said, "Fine." Each cop grabbed an arm, then casually hauled the drunk Mexican out of the building. As I started up the steps I felt slightly elated at having won the fight, but the headache and pain in my temple were pretty intense. I passed Johnny on the stairs, who gave me a sympathetic look.

"You must feel terrible," he said.

"No. It was kind of invigorating in its own way."

"What a man," said Johnny sarcastically.

I went into my apartment, took four aspirins, and smoked a joint. Touching the painful bruise, I winced, then smiled.

"You just can't beat the old headlock."

As I walked south on Van Ness, about two blocks from my place, I found a plaque on the wall of an apartment building. It was a cracked plaster bas-relief of Jack London in profile, with the inscription: "Jack London, world-famous novelist, journalist, short story writer, adventurer, war correspondent, and photoplay scenario writer, lived in this house during the 1914 production of William Selig's motion picture version of *The Sea Wolf*."

I was overwhelmed. "Jack London? Right here? In 1914? That's un-fucking-believable!"

I went directly to the Francis Howard Goldwyn (Sam's wife) Hollywood Library on Ivar Avenue and read Jack London's book *Call of the Wild*, which was terrific (I chose *Call of the Wild* instead of *The Sea Wolf* because it was much shorter). I then read up on Jack London. He'd gone to sea as a young man and traveled the world; had been a tramp who rode the rails, a longshoreman, and a miner in the Yukon during the Klondike gold rush; had published 50 books; and then had died at the age of 40 in 1916, two years after writing the photoplay scenario for *The Sea Wolf* in an apartment in Hollywood on Van Ness Avenue.

I thought, "Finding that plaque was an omen."

JANUARY 14, 1977

As I've been sitting here smoking pot and drinking beer an absolutely intriguing idea just occurred to me—ship out on a freighter to the Orient. It worked for Jack London and Joseph Conrad and Eugene O'Neill, why not me? See the world. Do some shit that's worth writing about.

*Now's the time to do something exciting, while I'm still
young. Live a little bit, then write about it.*

*I would have to put everything I own, including my au-
tomobile, somewhere. That is a lot of stuff, but not too
much, say to pawn off on dad's friend, Ralph. However he
doesn't have a basement, nor a large driveway.*

And there's some shit about seaman's papers.

Losing speed . . .

Puff . . .

ah . . .

. . .

. .

.

I had $500 in the bank and my own pound of weed, which also
had equity value—anytime I needed money I could just sell a bag.
So, I decided to quit my job at the deli, quit school, and finally get
serious about writing.

"I'm 18 already," I thought. "I've got to get on with it."

I purchased two reams (1,000 pages) of canary yellow erasable
typing paper at Bargain Circus, determined as hell to write something on every single page. As I walked out of the store, holding
the two boxes of paper in a plastic bag, I thought, "Within this
bag dwells a masterpiece, I just have to find it."

I had always read a lot, but now I began to read voraciously. I read
William Goldman's books *Temple of Gold* and *Boys and Girls Together*, and they both made me want to be a novelist. I read Jerzy
Kosinski's terrifying *The Painted Bird* and that totally freaked me
out. And having just read James Clavell's *Shogun* and *Tai-Pan*, I
followed up with *King Rat*, and that was terrific, too. I read *Mar-
jorie Morningstar* by Herman Wouk and just loved it. Then I took
on *The Idiot* by Fyodor Dostoyevsky and *The Heart of Darkness*
by Joseph Conrad and was seriously impressed by both.

One thing all of those authors had in common with each other,
but not with me, was that they had led lives that were worth writing about. They lived through the holocaust, served in WWII, were
incarcerated in Japanese prison camps, were condemned to death
and reprieved at the last second, and had sailed ships into the

heart of bloody darkness. What the hell had I ever done? Nothing. Oh, wait, that's right, I'd taken the GED test and graduated high school two years early. Wow!

I felt utterly ill-equipped for the job I was ostensibly taking on, and I kept thinking, "What's a good idea? What story can only *I* write? What matters to me? What means something?"

While waiting for a good idea, I wrote over a hundred pages of a novel, a fantasy love story about me and Renée, where she agrees to move to L.A., live with me, and attend UCLA. She and I continue to live in my apartment at 666 North Van Ness, and Renée (named Rona in the book) begins wandering around Hollywood with me at night, while making love to me all day long. After 100 pages of what clearly seemed like drivel even to me as I was writing it, I slowly came to realize that I had no story to tell, nor did I know what the hell I was writing. Reticently, I abandoned the novel. I'd never written anything that long before, so there was that—it was a pretty big stack of typed yellow paper. It also represented over two months of daily writing down the toilet. I concluded that I probably wasn't a novelist anyway, or at least not yet. Perhaps I'd have the wherewithal to become a novelist later in my life.

I'd been writing short stories regularly since junior high school, and so I kept right on doing it, only now they were on canary yellow paper. There was "Expectations," which was a short, Roald Dahl-like tale of a woman who hates her husband because he always does exactly the same thing every day, so she decides to kill him, and poisons his after-work drink. He comes home elated, with a big bump on my forehead, saying he hit his head on the way home and now sees what an asshole he's been, and it'll all be different now, then drinks the whole drink down and dies. As she cleans up she quips that things never turn out like she expects.

I wrote a series of weird, science-fiction, Harlan Ellison-esque stories, starting with "Rec-Room," an allegory about purgatory in an endless rec-room under construction; a story called "Johnnie," about a vague, ambitionless kid in the future, who is called before the authorities to explain his lack of ambition, and is then sentenced to life in suspended animation, with his brain simplified; and "Not To Be Reproduced," about a failed stand-up comic who was slowly, literally, disappearing until no one could hear him or see him and he no longer even had a reflection.

I then decided to do a screen adaptation of Kurt Vonnegut's book *Mother Night*, which I'd read three times and loved. I knew I didn't have the rights, but I decided to do it anyway, for the experience. However, within 25 pages I was more confused than I'd ever been about anything I'd ever tried to write before—I couldn't see how this book could *ever* be a movie. Yet, my inspiration for attempting the adaptation was *Slaughterhouse-Five*, which had clearly been adapted for the screen, and beautifully, too. Sadly, I put this project aside, too.

Throughout all of this I kept writing a lot of poetry. For some reason poetry seemed to come the easiest to me, although I obsessively wrote and rewrote each poem over and over again by hand, then finally typed them up. I loved rhyme and meter, even if they weren't hip to use in poetry anymore. But every time I experimented with free-form, non-rhyming poetry it felt like a big cop-out. I liked to use the movie industry as my subject matter.

> *The Director*
> *"Come on, let's move, let's start the show,"*
> *The director did decree.*
> *"Actors in places and ready to go?*
> *We'll start at the count of three."*
>
> *"Ready!" cried camera, "Speed!" cried sound,*
> *"Okay," the director replied.*
> *"Ready and action!" he yelled with a bound,*
> *And the producer hopefully sighed.*
>
> *Take one, take two, take three, take four,*
> *It never turns out right.*
> *The actors return and try once more,*
> *The director's will their plight.*
>
> *Lights burn hotter, make-up smears,*
> *The lines begin to fade.*
> *They stagger forth, but barely hear*
> *The call the director bade.*

"Print it and let's break for lunch,
The scene worked out just fine.
Be back at one, I've got a hunch
We'll all go home on time."

Mumbling mumbles and wiping my head,
The editor stepped to day.
"The film is finished" he quietly said,
"I hope it looks OK."

The lights went down, the curtains fold,
The credits then appear.
The film's great power then took hold,
The audience voiced a cheer.

The director sighed and walked away,
The theater left behind.
"The film's so good they'll raise my pay,
And then they'll steal my mind."

I wrote quite a few poems, laboring over each of one. I had to finally conclude, though, that in the present day and age there probably wasn't much of a future in being a poet, even as a sidelight. Nor was it humanly possible to make a living writing short stories anymore (not that I'd sold one yet anyway). Therefore, I decided it was time to get down to it and write a screenplay. Something commercial that would sell.

Wandering the streets of Hollywood at night, I thought and thought, "What's a good idea? What's a saleable idea? And just because it's seemingly saleable now, will it be in a year or two?"

I finally decided to write a very violent feature screenplay called *The Prey*. The story, set during the American Civil War, was about a homicidal bounty hunter who can no longer find prey big enough or wild enough in America, so he goes to Africa on a safari. His indiscriminate killing of every animal he encounters so utterly offends the African native bearers in his safari that they hold a big religious service, chanting their ancient songs to the gods, which eventually causes all of the animals of the jungle to attack the bounty hunter and rip him to shreds. I was so paranoid that whoever would ultimately direct the film based on my script might not shoot it properly—that is, as I imagined it—that I meticulously wrote in every single camera angle. The screenwriting books said not to do that, but fuck 'em! What did they know?

Example:

> 232.   LONG SHOT – SAFARI
>
> Chanting can be heard and gets louder as the safari approaches.
>
> 233.   MED. CU – KOTUBA
>
> He chants in a grumbling wail that the rest of the men follow.
>
> 234.   MED. CU – BURROUGHS
>
> He is very mad, but holds it in check.

Etc., etc., etc.

This took another two months of writing all night long every night. A feature-length screenplay is usually about 120 pages. That generally translates into a two-hour movie, at approximately a minute a page. When I was done with screenplay of *The Prey* it only came out to 39 pages. I was stunned. How could that be? It seemed like a full-length movie to me. After serious deliberation, I decided that it had to be that the margins were simply too wide. I retyped the entire script with narrower margins and it came out to 52 pages. At a minute a page, that wasn't even an hour.

"If it's not even an hour long, then it's not feature-length," I said incredulously. "What the hell is going on?"

I gave the script out to several people, including my dad's friend, Ralph, and a guy from Sherwood Oaks, and they both hated it. They didn't *dislike* it, they *hated* it, and both said that they found it pretty much unreadable.

To save money during these months spent intensively writing, I ate only the store brand macaroni and cheese that cost 15 cents a box. After four or five months of this diet, I noticed that my gums were bleeding a lot when I brushed my teeth. When the bleeding wouldn't stop, and all of my teeth began feeling loose, not to mention that I was also consistently feeling strangely light-headed, I finally decided it was time to see a doctor.

I went to the local free clinic a block down on Van Ness where I saw an eager white, female doctor in her late 20s. I told her my gums were bleeding, my teeth felt like they were going to fall out, and that I'd seemingly lost my equilibrium.

She immediately asked, "What do you eat?"

"Well, Buckwheats cereal in the morning, and generally macaroni and cheese for dinner."

"Uh-huh?"

I thought for a second. "That's pretty much it. Oh, TV dinners, sometimes."

"No fruit? No vegetables?"

"Uh-uh. Unless there's vegetables in the TV dinner. Although I sometimes throw those out."

As she poked around in my mouth with her rubber-gloved finger her expression became truly befuddled, then slightly horrified.

Shaking her head in disgust and pulling off the rubber gloves, she said, "You've got scurvy. I've never actually seen a case of it before, I've only read about it. It's what sailors used to get on ships before they discovered vitamin C. But then about a hundred and fifty years ago they began eating lemons and limes and that cured it. That's why British sailors were called 'Limeys,' by the way, because they smelled like limes."

I said, "That's fascinating."

The doctor pointed her finger directly into my face. "You need to take vitamin C, drink orange juice, and eat fruit and vegetables. You understand?"

I nodded, "Yeah."

I immediately began taking vitamin C and drinking orange juice, and the problem cleared right up. My gums quit bleeding, my teeth stopped feeling loose, and the light-headedness went away.

I thought, "Hmmm, maybe since I now personally understand the problem, I should write a story about sailors, who all get scurvy, go crazy and kill each other . . ." But I didn't do it.

My apartment, meanwhile, had a major cockroach problem, although luckily the larger bugs stayed in the bathroom. Since I didn't like killing them, I would use the plant sprayer set on "stream," like squirt gun, and propel the roaches back down the drain, then turn on the faucet and wash them further down. It was a never ending battle. It kept reminding me of an episode of *Night*

Gallery where Patrick O'Neal washes a spider down the drain, but it keeps crawling back up bigger each time.

One night while standing in the bathroom urinating, the orange juice can sitting on the floor beneath the toilet to catch the water dripping from the pipe began shaking and making a little clattering noise. As I stood there with my dick in my hand, wondering what the hell was going on, I finally realized I was experiencing my first earthquake. It was really wild, and I dug it.

"*Whoa!*"

On occasion Marvis would join me on my midnight walks through Hollywood. Marvis said, "If you keep your eyes peeled for money, sometimes you find it. And in lieu of money, long cigarette butts are good, too."

So we'd wander up and down Hollywood Boulevard looking for money and long cigarette butts. We actually did find a few coins here and there, but not much. We never found any bills. When we found a long butt, we'd break off the filter, light it up and share it.

"My mother is a big woman," said Marvis, "and incredibly overbearing. She dressed me in a little suit coat, with a bowtie and a briefcase throughout my youth. I was the school geek. She always demanded that I get nothing less than As. If I ever got a B, god forbid, she'd hit me on the back of the hand with a hairbrush. Hard. So, as soon as I finished college I got the hell out of Cleveland as fast as I could, and I came to Hollywood. And here I am, wandering up Hollywood Boulevard in the middle of the night searching for long cigarette butts."

I said, "Yeah, but *I'm* having a good time."

Marvis nodded. "Yeah, me, too."

> *DECEMBER 31ˢᵗ, 1976-77*
>
> *It's New Year's Eve. I'm 18 years old, drunk on beer, stoned on pot, free, white, unemployed, and living in Hollywood. I was actually able to buy beer with my new fake ID I purchased from an ad in the back of the LA Weekly. Ten dollars well spent.*
>
> *What will this new year hold in store for me?*

My dad hadn't called me once in six months. He and I had spoken briefly a few times when I'd called, although I usually just ended up talking to my mom. My mom wasn't being terribly friendly, either. Clearly, they both disapproved of my being in Hollywood.

When I called home this time I specifically asked to speak with my dad.

"Hello?"

"Hi, dad."

"Hi, Josh. What's up?"

"Oh, you know. This and that. How's everyone?"

"Fine. Everything going all right?"

"Fine."

"How's your car?" my dad asked, as he always did.

"Fine."

"How's school?"

"Fine, uh . . ."

"Yeah?"

"Could I borrow some money?"

"Why?"

"'Cause I'm almost out."

"What happened to working?"

"I've stopped for a while so I can concentrate on writing. Writing is work."

"Except no one's paying you."

"Yeah, but if I keep at it and actually get good at it, maybe someone will."

"But no one's paying you now."

"No."

"And now you want to borrow money?"

"Uh-huh."

"Well, to borrow money you'd need collateral. What have you got?"

I was stumped. "Uh, my car."

"I think you need that."

"Yeah, I guess I do."

"So?"

"So, I guess I don't have any other collateral."

"Then I guess you can't borrow any money."

I sighed. "Okay, how about you just *give* me some money?"

"I don't just *give* money."

"Okay, then, it was great talking to you."

"You, too."

"'Bye."

"Bye-bye."

We hung up.

When I lit a cigarette I found that my hand was shaking. I flicked the spent match out the open window and shook my head.

"*What a fuckin' asshole!*"

So, I began selling off little bits of my precious pound of weed. A quarter of an ounce here, then a quarter of an ounce there, and I somehow managed to get by.

An ad on the rock & roll radio station KROQ said that if you wanted to be an extra in John Cassavetes's new film, *Opening Night*, go to the Pasadena Auditorium on January 19th wearing dress clothes, and you'd also get a free lunch, but no pay. I thought, "That's the best offer I've heard yet," so I dressed up in a suit and tie and went.

There were several hundred other people there and we all sat in the audience clapping all day long while watching John Cassavetes and Gena Rowlands perform a scene from a fake play within the movie that ended with each of them reaching back and grabbing their own ankles. By lunch my hands were bright red and aching. Nevertheless, unlike many of the other extras I might add, I went back in for the second half of the day and clapped until my hands were swollen and throbbing. When I got into my car to drive home that night I could not make a fist or tightly grab the steering wheel with either hand. I had to drive by pressing my arms against the wheel.

A few days later I received a call from an assistant director asking if I'd like to do some more extra work on *Opening Night*. I immediately said, "Sure." Luckily, the next location was much closer to my apartment. It was at the American Theater on Wilshire Boulevard between La Brea Avenue and Vine Street, about two miles away. It was a night shoot and I was instructed to be there at 5:00 P.M. wearing an overcoat.

As the crew set up outside the theater, the extras, all dressed in warm coats since it was supposed to be New York in the winter, did nothing but hang around the front of the theater for the next five hours. I attempted to strike up a conversation with a German fellow who apparently had absolutely nothing to say about anything. I asked if he liked any German films and the guy shrugged. I said, "Fassbinder? Herzog? Wim Wenders? Fritz Lang?"

Nothing.

A sandy-haired, bespectacled, collegiate-looking fellow of 25, wearing a long wool coat, stepped up and said, "I've seen all those guy's films."

I said skeptically, "*All* of them?"

He nodded. "Pretty much."

"What do you mean *exactly*?"

"I mean, I've seen *all* of Wim Wenders' films, *all* of Werner Herzog's films, nearly all of Fritz Lang's films, although I'm still missing a few of his early silents, and I've seen every Fassbinder film that's been released in the United States, but there are several that haven't been released here yet. I think German cinema is very interesting these days, what do you think?"

"I do, too," I said. "Although, quite frankly, Fassbinder bores me. I do like Herzog, though, particularly *The Enigma of Kasper Hauser*."

The fellow smiled. "Yes, that was very good. My name's Rick Sandford."

"Josh Becker," I said, putting out my hand. Rick shook my hand and I thought, "Oh, he's gay, too."

Rick asked, "What's your favorite movie?"

Stalling, I replied, "The ones I've seen the most are *Play It Again, Sam* and *The Godfather*. Fourteen times for *Play It Again, Sam* and 12 times for *The Godfather*. Ten for *Godfather II*."

Rick grinned. He was impressed. "But what's your *favorite* film?"

I sighed. Good question. Finally . . .

"*The Magnificent Ambersons* or *The Bridge on the River Kwai*, how about you?"

Rick grinned. "Not *Kane*, huh?"

I shrugged, "I love *Citizen Kane*, don't get me wrong, but I like *Ambersons* better."

Rick nodded. "I agree."

I imitated Ray Collins from *The Magnificent Ambersons*, "By Jove, Georgie, you *are* a puzzle."

Rick imitated Tim Holt, "I will be shot. I will."

We both laughed.

Rick said, "My favorite film is *2001: A Space Odyssey*. I've seen it 28 times, in the theater, all in 70mm. It is sublime."

I nodded, very impressed. I thought seeing a movie 14 times in the theater was pretty obsessive, but I knew nothing about movie obsession compared to Rick.

We talked movies nonstop all night long during shooting, then went back to my place, talked movies all day, then they went back to the set and continued shooting and talked movies all through the next night, too. Not only were John Cassavetes and Gena Rowlands in these scenes, but so were Joan Blondell from the '30s Cagney movies, and Paul Stewart, who was actually in *Citizen Kane*.

At dawn, after two entire nights and one whole day of nonstop movie talk, Rick and I ended up at Rick's place. He lived in a bungalow behind a house in West Hollywood. A decaying red VW bug with flat tires was parked on the grass in front of his door. Inside it was actually quite a spacious bungalow, although every piece of clothing Rick owned was strewn across every single surface of the place. Rick had abandoned the kitchen at some point months before, once he'd used every dish, and a swarm of fruit flies circled around over the sink. I opened the door and looked in. Rick said, "I don't go in there. Just shut the door. Did I mention that I'm being evicted."

I nodded, "I wonder why? Is that your Volkswagen out there?"

"Yes, but I don't drive. I don't have a driver's license, or a bank account, or a credit card, either."

"Good thinking."

Rick tossed away some clothes, unburied a record player, and put on the soundtrack album of *Taxi Driver* by Bernard Herrmann. It's a great score, but it sounded just awful.

I wrinkled my brow. "What's wrong with it?"

"What do you mean?" asked Rick, sitting down on the bed.

"It sounds terrible."

"Really? In what way?"

I said, "In an audio kind of way." I inspected the cheap little stereo and found that there was a glob of dust on the needle the size of a gumball. I plucked it off, then set the needle back on the record—it now sounded 50 percent better.

Rick's face lit up like he'd just witnessed a miracle. "You *fixed* it."

I still didn't think it sounded all that good. I dug through more clothes to the back of the stereo and found that one of the speakers wasn't plugged in. I plugged it in, and suddenly all the rest of the instruments could be heard. Now it at least sounded normal.

Once again, Rick was utterly thrilled. He clasped his hands together in joy. "Oh my god, it sounds *great!*"

"Yeah, for a 10-dollar stereo."

I sat down on the foot of the bed and lit a cigarette.

The room was cloaked in a gray early morning half-light. The smoke from my cigarette hung in the air. Rick was leaning back against the pillows and headboard, nervously jiggling his foot, causing the whole bed to shake and squeak.

Rick said, "I'm gay you know."

I said, "I know."

Rick looked slightly alarmed. "How did you know?"

I shrugged. "I just knew. From the first second I met you."

Rick looked intrigued. "Really?"

"Uh-huh."

"So?"

"So, what?"

"So, you wanna have sex?"

I shook my head. "No. I'm not gay."

Rick smiled. "But you could start."

"No thanks."

We sat in silence for a moment. Rick continued jiggling his foot and the bed continued to shake and squeak. Finally . . .

"Am I making you nervous?" asked Rick.

"Yes," I said.

"Why?"

"Well, you are *writhing* there on the bed."

Rick said very calmly, "You call *this* writhing? Give me a chance and I'll show you *writhing*."

We both burst out laughing and the tension was broken.

Sounding rather unsure, Rick asked, "So, what is it then? You want to be 'friends'?"

I shrugged, "Sure."

Rick rubbed his chin in befuddlement. "I've never had a straight friend before. What would we do?"

"Well, we could probably go to the movies together."

Rick nodded. "Yeah, I guess we could do that."

I shrugged, "Look, we may not have sex, but we'll always have the movies, and Paris."

Rick smiled. "You know too much about movies to not be gay. You wanna smoke some pot?"

I grinned, "Now you're talkin' my language."

As we smoked a joint, Rick showed me his file of carbon copies of letters he had written to movie stars and directors, as well as all of their replies. He'd written to seemingly everybody, and many had actually answered him, too. Rick believed the reason that he got responses was because he wrote 10-to-30-page in-depth studies of their entire careers. "How could they possibly ignore it?" he said. I read Rick's 25-page letter to Gena Rowlands, written immediately after he'd seen *A Woman Under the Influence* and was deeply moved by her performance. Rick's letter wasn't some insignificant piece of fan mail; this was a serious piece of analytical writing, and Rick was clearly a very good writer. Oddly, his typewriter wrote in script.

I said, "I loved *A Woman Under the Influence*, too. I won an award for my review of it in the college newspaper."

Rick said, "I'd love to read it."

"Sure," I said, immediately knowing I'd never show it to Rick because, having just read Rick's writing, my writing now seemed painfully amateurish, particularly from two years ago.

When I finally left Rick's place, after at least 40 hours of non-stop movie talk, as well as two long chilly nights of extra work, I felt like I was tripping on acid. All the colors seemed heightened, and the bright areas were leaving trails.

Strangely, I knew that Rick was now one of my best friends, and always would be.

The *Opening Night* A.D. called me back in for another day of extra work, but they didn't call Rick. This was apparently based on zip codes and proximity to the new location, which was a restaurant in downtown L.A. All of the scenes were being shot inside the restaurant between Gena Rowlands and Ben Gazzara, who were both sitting in a booth with their backs to a big window. Since this was supposed to be New York in the winter, the people passing back and forth outside the window, including me, had to be dressed appropriately in coats, scarves and gloves. An A.D. was stationed at either side of the window, choosing which extras to send through and when. Being a ham deep in my heart, every time I went through and suspected I'd be seen on camera between the two actors, I'd shiver and shake my arms like I was freezing (it was probably about 85 degrees out). The A.D.s loved my little performance and sent me back through over and over again. Each time I'd do a little variation on my frozen routine, and each time the A.D.s would smile in approval, then send me back through again.

Lunch that day was served inside the restaurant. I saw Gena Rowlands sitting all by herself in a booth. Strangely, no one was eating with her. I summoned up all of my courage, walked over and asked, "Do you mind if I sit down?"

She shrugged, "No. Go ahead."

I told her that I had written a very positive review of *A Woman Under the Influence* for my college newspaper at Eastern Michigan University a few years earlier and had won an award for the best article of the month. She smiled weakly.

After a long moment of uncomfortable silence, I said, "My friend, Rick Sandford, wrote you a very long, typed fan letter a few years ago analyzing your entire career. Do you remember it? His typewriter types in script."

Without any hesitation Ms. Rowlands reached into her purse and retrieved Rick's letter, all dog-eared and clearly having been read many times. She held it up and said, "This one?"

I was astounded. "Yeah, that one."

Gena Rowlands nodded. "It's a good letter," and she put it back in her purse.

Having indeed been evicted from his bungalow in West Hollywood, Rick Sandford and his best friend, Stacey, with whom he had grown up in Reno, and her big dog all moved into a one-bedroom apartment at 666 North Van Ness, next door to Nate. Stacey was a smart, slim, boyish lesbian. Soon thereafter, Stacey's lover, Krista, came to stay for a while, too. She wore a foot-long Bowie knife on her belt, and she also had a big dog. The small one-bedroom apartment immediately became a total madhouse.

Rick began hanging out at my place as much as humanly possible.

I asked Rick, "Would you like a cup of coffee?"

Rick said, "Sure. Procreation is a sin."

I filled the kettle in the bathroom. "Excuse me?"

Rick repeated, "Procreation is a sin. Humans are smarter than animals; we don't have to have children just because we have sex."

"Certainly not you," I said.

"No, of course, not me. I mean, heterosexuals, like you."

"Right. Okay." I served the instant coffee (with three spoonfuls for each cup), then sat down and rolled a joint.

Rick concluded, "So procreation is a sin."

"A sin? Don't you think that's a tad extreme?"

Rick gulped his coffee and got excited. "No, I don't! Don't you see, this is the worst of all possible worlds!"

I lit the joint, took a big hit and handed it to Rick.

"It is?"

"Yes. Clearly." Rick took a hit, then another gulp of coffee and said, "Hey, that's pretty good, for instant." He blew out the smoke. "Yes, the worst of all possible worlds." He handed me back the joint.

I took it and chuckled. "You're shittin' me, right?"

"No," said Rick, dead serious.

"Rick, is your rent paid?"

"Yes."

"Okay. So is mine. And we're both sitting here on a Tuesday afternoon, smokin' a doob, drinkin' coffee, with our rent paid. We're not living in mud huts with our animals; we're not at Auschwitz; it's not the Inquisition; there's no Black Plague. How is this *possibly* the worst of all possible worlds?

Rick was getting agitated. "Because there were never this many people on the planet before."

"So what?"

"So, we're using everything up, and destroying the environment!"

"But at this present moment it's not all used up. And procreation isn't a sin—I think it may just be the whole point of why we're here. Y'know, continuation of the species, and all that."

"But we don't *have* to! We have bigger brains! We have free will!"

I waved my hand dismissively. "Humans are no different than worms or bugs. Procreation is the point of existence. All this other stuff, like art and philosophy and literature and movies are just to kid us into believing that life means something more than procreation, but in fact it doesn't."

Rick slammed his coffee cup down on the table so hard it spilled. He stood up and pointed down at me.

"We can't be friends; we have nothing in common!"

I smiled. "What about all those movies? And Paris? Look, we're friends now, Rick, and there's nothing you can do about it."

"*Oh, bullshit!*"

Rick stomped out of the apartment.

I grinned, toasting up the roach.

Rick and I began going to the movies together all the time. We frequently went to the Vagabond Theater on Wilshire Boulevard and Vermont, the oldest revival house in town with the most uncomfortable seats. We saw *The Member of the Wedding* with Julie Harris, Ethel Waters, and Brandon DeWilde, which we'd both seen before. The movie was so good, and moved us both so much that we just sat through it a second time, in those painful, horrible seats.

As we walked the several miles home, we kept repeating lines from the film.

"Do not try to capture me," said Rick.

"Well, the party's over, and the monkey's dead," I said.

Rick did Ethel Waters, "Oh, this ol' glass eye don't do me no seein' good at all."

We both burst out laughing, feeling great. What could be better than seeing a movie you absolutely loved, twice, with someone else who loved it just as much as you, maybe more? Nothing, that's what.

What I found slightly disturbing, though, about hanging around with Rick was that after a few months I could feel myself potentially *becoming* Rick—an obsessed, extreme *filmgoer*, not a *filmmaker*. I loved going to the movies, but I sure as hell didn't want to become just one more nutty moviegoer in Hollywood, that was for damn sure.

I shook my fist at the heavens. "As God is my witness, if it's the last thing I fucking do, I'm going to be a film director. And a screenwriter, too, goddamnit!

> *"FEBRUARY 6, 1977*
> *I have neglected my journal for quite some time now. I had a reason for doing this (I'm very high right now and having trouble typing); maybe, if I wasn't fulfilling my writing habit with the journal I might write some good stuff.*
>
> *Well . . . I've started some good things, I think, but by the time I finish them they're apparently no longer any good."*

A Valentine's Day card arrived from Renée, postmarked Detroit, MI 10 Feb, 1977. It was purple, and it pictured a sad little person leaning against a broken heart, with "Help!" written in the crack of the heart. The front of the card read, "Before I met you, I was floundering in the depths of depression and didn't know what was going on . . ." Then inside the card it said, " . . . Now I'm fluttering in the heights of delirium . . . and I still don't know what's going on?!! Happy Valentine's Day, Love Renée."

Frowning, I tossed the card in the bottom drawer of the desk.

One afternoon I came into Rick and Stacey's apartment, which was in such disarray it looked like a bomb had exploded inside, to find Rick battling Stacey's dog with a broom. Rick had the dog pushed into a corner where it was growling and snapping at the broom's bristles.

Rick stated, "I hate this dog, and this dog hates me!"

I shut the door and went back to my own apartment.

I asked both Rick and Stacey to read *The Prey*. They both promptly read it and they both seriously, and sincerely, *hated* it.

Rick said as snidely as was humanly possible, "Have you ever heard of the word *cliché?*"

Stacey said, "It's like a stupid, idiotic, horror version of *Roots*. Is that how you meant it?"

On Friday, March 11th, Rick and I attended the opening of Filmex, the 1977 Los Angeles International Film Exposition, that began with the premiere of Woody Allen's newest film, *Annie Hall*. Woody wasn't there, but Diane Keaton was. The film was utterly brilliant, totally hysterical, and Rick and I both laughed until we hurt. We fully realized that we had just seen the very first screening of a classic film, and the film to beat for Best Picture.

The finale of Filmex '77 was a 54-hour musical marathon. Rick had scored some speed and I brought the weed. The first film of the marathon was *The Wizard of Oz,* introduced by the film's producer, Mervyn LeRoy, the same guy who directed *Little Caesar* with Edward G. Robinson in 1930, and *I Am a Fugitive from a Chain Gang* with Paul Muni in 1932. I couldn't fucking believe I was in the same room as the living, breathing Mervyn LeRoy. It was incredible!

Rick and I settled back in our seats and watched in a row: *The Wizard of Oz, Roberta, The Kid from Spain, Cabin in the Sky, West Side Story, Oklahoma!, My Fair Lady, Yankee Doodle Dandy, Dumbo, The Big Broadcast, Cover Girl, Belle of the Nineties, Meet Me in St. Louis, Let the Good Times Roll, Footlight Parade, Pajama Game, King of Burlesque, The Beggar's Opera,* and *It's Always Fair Weather*. For two entire days and nights we watched musicals, ate speed, popcorn, candy, drank Coke, and every few hours ducked out to my car in the parking structure to smoke more dope. We would then drag our weary asses, numbed brains, and bugging eyes, back in for more musicals.

When we finally left, eight hours short of the full 54, both of us were totally sick to our stomachs, had roaring headaches, and could barely see through eyes that were not only bloodshot, but sunken and crossed. We looked like zombies from *Night of the Living Dead*. It was a perilous journey up Olympic Boulevard in the bright California sunshine since I truly could not see. Technicolor movies had damaged my optic nerves.

To my great relief, at the end of the month both Rick and Stacey moved out.

Rick got a place in West Hollywood, on Alta Vista Boulevard, a few blocks behind the Formosa Café and Samuel Goldwyn Studio, where they shot *The Best Years of Our Lives*.

As I got about three-quarters of the way through writing all over the 1,000 yellow pages of paper, it very slowly dawned on me that I really had no fucking clue what I was doing. My novel, that seemed nothing like a novel, was obviously utter crap. Everyone *hated* my screenplay, that didn't even look like a screenplay, and was only 52 pages.

I shook my head, "What am I thinking? Those two things represent over four months of my life."

As I walked and paced and slept and jacked off and ate macaroni and cheese and washed it down with frozen concentrate orange juice, I thought and thought: How to proceed? I felt like a rat stuck in the corner of a maze. But how did one even go about turning oneself around to look for a way out, let alone finding it?

The answer that finally occurred to me was *size*. These projects had all simply been too big for me to handle just yet. I needed to write something short and make it work before I would be in a position to graduate up to longer things, like feature-length screenplays and novels. Hell, my short stories were okay. Maybe they weren't great, but they weren't bad. So why not work from there?

Okay. So next I set myself the task of writing a short screenplay, one that I could potentially shoot in Super 8. But more than that, a short screenplay that functioned as a screenplay, and as a story. It would be 20 or 25 minutes, which is plenty of time to tell a whole story. Having attended the Ann Arbor Super 8 Film Festival a few times, I knew very well that five to ten minutes could seem like an eternity when there's no story, or a bad story, as most of the films in the festival proved over and over again.

Then, after seeing both *Annie Hall* and *Rocky*, each for the fourth time, at the second-run theater The Gordon (owned by Lou from the Encore), I had an earthshaking idea, "What about a boxing comedy?" I came up with a boxing tale about a Woody Allen-ish schnook who gets a shot at the world heavyweight championship that I entitled *The Final Round*. The only tricky aspect would be getting the use of a boxing ring, but otherwise the rest of the story was nothing more than people in rooms talking to each other, and that didn't seem particularly difficult. I could immediately imagine the guys I knew back in Michigan, Sam Raimi, Scott Spiegel, and Bruce Campbell, in the various parts. Sadly, that did me no good at all stuck there in L.A.

Could I get people in L.A. to help me the way those guys had back in Michigan? People in L.A. didn't seem to have the slightest interest in working in the lowly gauge of Super 8, which was basically treated like it was beneath contempt. Nor could I afford to shoot in 16mm at the moment, either. But, no question about it, I just *had* to make another movie.

So I decided to shoot an even shorter, easier film in Super 8, about five minutes long, starring only myself and Rick Sandford, who was more than happy to have a speaking part in a movie. Rick played his role with a passable British accent, too (he said he was imitating Richard Burton, but I don't think he sounded anything like him). The film was based on a short short story called "The Choice" by W. Hilton-Jacobs.

Two men are in a beautiful living room. Man #1 (Rick) sets down a silver tray with a coffee pot and two cups. Man #2 (me in a yellow Hawaiian shirt) stands up holding a tape recorder, a pad and pen, with a camera around my neck, and says, "Well, off to the future," and disappears. Man #2 reappears one second later, hair sticking up, clothes dirty and wrinkled, still holding the pad, tape recorder and the camera. Man #2 sits down. Man #1 looks at him expectantly.

MAN #1: So?

MAN #2: So, how about that coffee?

Man #1 pours Man #2 a cup of coffee, which he happily drinks.

MAN #1: So, you've been in the future for what could amount to years. So what happened? What did you see?

Man #2 slowly drinks the coffee, then sets down the cup.

MAN #2: Well, I can't remember anything.

MAN #1: But what about your camera? The notes? The tape recorder?

Man #1 looks and there are no notes in the pad, no pictures have been taken, nor has the tape recorder been used.

MAN #1 (exasperated): You don't remember anything?

MAN #2: Wait, I do remember one thing—I was shown everything, and I was told everything. I was then asked if I wanted to remember or not?

MAN #1: And you chose not to?

MAN #2: I don't remember.

MAN #1: How extraordinary!

The end.

However, as many people as I called—Marvis was still working on *Super Train*, Sherman was both working and in school—I could only get one person to show up and help. Then I only had use of the location for a few hours, I didn't bring enough extension cords, the lights blew the circuit breakers, and I was also supposed to light, direct, *and* give some sort of performance? It was a total bloody nightmare.

Surprise, surprise, the film turned out rather poorly, too. The sound mysteriously had a loud buzz in it, the lighting was flat and ugly, both the direction and the cutting were awkward, and it was only about five fucking minutes long, for Christ's sake! How the hell was I going to make *The Final Round*, which would probably run 20 to 25 minutes?

I couldn't, that's what.

It seemed that the harder I tried, the worse things turned out and the more confused I became.

I thought, "I can't make this work. I can't make *anything* work. What's wrong with me?"

In the late afternoon of March 28th, Rick and I attended an Oscar party at Sherman's apartment on Sixth Street. Sherman and I had spoken on the phone many times at great length over the past few months, but had never actually met. Rick and I stepped up and I knocked on the door. The door opened and there stood a short, thin, wiry fellow of 26, with a dark complexion, black curly hair, and a black mustache. I was completely taken aback.

"*Sherman?*" I asked incredulously.

"*Josh?*" said Sherman, every bit as amazed.

"You don't look *anything* like you're supposed to."

"Yeah? Well, neither do you."

We both started to laugh and shook hands.

I said, "Sherman, this is Rick. Rick, Sherman."

Rick shook Sherman's hand saying, "Nice to meet you."

Sherman said, "Come on in. Have a drink. Take a load off. Watch the Oscars. Who do you think will win?"

I unhesitatingly said, "*Rocky.*"

Rick said, "*Taxi Driver ought* to win."

Sherman and I both simultaneously said, "Sure, it *ought* to . . ." then we both burst out laughing again.

"Jinx," I said.

Sherman and I hit it off instantly.

The 49th annual Oscar telecast was particularly weird. The Oscars had been stumbling around blindly for the past several years, ever since Bob Hope had retired from hosting the show. Instead of replacing him, though, they kept getting multiple hosts. This year the hosts were Richard Pryor, Ellen Burstyn, Warren Beatty, and Jane Fonda. Oddly, they had hired William Friedkin, director of *The French Connection* and *The Exorcist*, to direct the show to supposedly make it "hipper." As usual, however, the Academy had no idea what hip was, and the show came off as a mish-mosh of weird, inappropriate, uncomfortable moments, like a giant King Kong hand awkwardly delivering one of the envelopes, or Sylvester Stallone fake sparring with a befuddled-looking Muhammad Ali.

When the Best Actor Oscar went to the recently-deceased Peter Finch for *Network*, instead of Finch's black, Jamaican wife being called up to receive the award, the film's writer, Paddy Chayefsky, was called up, causing a moment of complete hushed outrage in the audience. Paddy Chayefsky brilliantly saved the moment by immediately introducing Peter Finch's wife, bringing her up on stage and giving her the award. This was followed by a standing ovation that was by far the best moment of the night.

When *Rocky* won Best Picture, Rick was so disgusted that he proclaimed, "*Ridiculous!*" stood up, and walked right out the open front door without looking back. I was incredulous. I imitated Jack

Benny, "Well!" Sherman seemed highly amused, puffing on a cigar.

"What's with him?" asked Sherman.

I shrugged. "He really didn't like *Rocky*."

Sherman rolled the cigar between my fingers. "Huh. He's gay, right?"

I nodded. "Yeah."

"Are you?"

"No. Are you?"

"No. My girlfriend lives upstairs. So, how did you meet Rick?"

"We were both extras on John Cassavetes' new film, *Opening Night*."

"Well that's pretty cool."

"I liked *Rocky*," I said. "I saw it six times. I'd love to make a movie that good, and that cheap. At $1 million, it's now theoretically the cheapest Best Picture ever, with inflation. The cheapest is really *Marty*, which was like $800,000, but that was in 1955 dollars."

Sherman nodded, "James Crabe, the director of photography, spoke to my cinematography class at AFI. I think he made terrific use of the Steadicam."

"Yeah, me, too. That scene where Rocky is running as fast as he can along the waterfront was incredible."

"Yeah, it was."

We both nodded in accord, blowing smoke to the center of the room.

After a moment Sherman leaned forward, grinned maniacally, and said, "Guess what?"

I shrugged. "What?"

Sherman looked all around to make sure the coast was clear, then said, "I'm tripping my fucking brains out."

I was amazed. "Really? I had no idea. All this time?"

Sherman nodded, "Yeah, all this time. I've got a whole bunch of window pane in the fridge, if you're ever interested."

I shrugged. "Okay. Not tonight, though."

Sherman leaned back and puffed on his cigar. "No, some other time."

I looked closer at Sherman's eyes and they nothing but dilated pupil.

"You *are* tripping."

Sherman nodded, "I sure am."

As I walked south down Van Ness a few blocks from my place, just past the Jack London plaque, I would often hear a rollicking, barrel-house piano coming from inside a closed garage facing the street. Several times I stopped for a moment and listened because it was so good.

One day as I walked by and I once again heard the piano music, I found that the garage door was open. Inside the garage, exuberantly pounding the ivories was a round-faced black fellow in his late -20s/early-30s wearing a bathrobe. I stopped right outside the garage, where the piano-player could see me, and happily listened to the music. The guy was really terrific. When the song ended, I applauded.

"That was great!" I said.

"Thank you, thank you," said the pianist, bowing at the waist.

"My name's Josh, I live just up the street."

"I'm Cecil," he said, shaking my hand vigorously.

I thought, "Oh my God, a heterosexual. What's he doing here?"

I asked, "Do you write songs?"

Cecil nodded. "Sure. I'm a songwriter, musician, *and* a security guard."

"Do you write lyrics, too?"

"Yeah. Some."

"Y'know, I write poetry, and a few of my poems were actually written to be lyrics. Would you like to see them?"

"Sure. You wanna smoke a joint?"

"Yeah, I would."

"Then shut the garage door."

I shut the garage door.

The next time I heard the piano music as I was walking by, I went home and got a few of my poems. I walked back down the block toward the music, then knocked on the closed garage door.

"*Entré*," came Cecil's voice from within.

I swung open the door and there sat Cecil behind the piano, in the same bathrobe and engulfed in a cloud of pot smoke, a big fat joint in his mouth. I entered holding several sheets of yellow paper.

Cecil smiled, "Shut the door and we will imbibe."

I shut the door. Cecil toasted up the fat joint, took a big hit and handed it to me. I also took a big hit and held it in.

Cecil pointed at the yellow papers. "What have you there?"

I held up the papers and blew out the smoke. "Lyrics. Or, more precisely, poems that could be lyrics, I think."

Reaching out, Cecil said, "Let me see."

I handed them over. "Particularly the top one. 'Technicolor Blues.' It was written as a song."

Cecil slowly read it, occasionally nodding his head, hitting the joint and letting the smoke go up his nose.

Technicolor Blues

The lights are hot
Your makeup smears,
You work all day
For forty years

Your words are canned,
And life is trash,
But you're always there
Cause you need the cash

Oh, they steal your face,
And they steal your soul,
Gone without a trace,
'Fore the cameras roll.

Right or left or up or down
Don't matter how you choose.
Dissolve right in or fade right out
Those Technicolor blues.

It repeated this structure for three more verses, then one more chorus.

After several minutes, Cecil set the papers on the piano's music stand. With the lit joint in the corner of his mouth, he poised his fingers over the keyboard. I became almost giddy with excitement as I watched, and participated in, the collaborative process of songwriting. Meanwhile, Cecil absently hit a dissonant chord, then frowned. He hit another off-key chord, then sadly shook his head. He suddenly grabbed all the sheets of yellow paper off the piano's music stand, and handed them back to me.

"No, that won't work."

I was horrified, blushing all the way to the tops of my ears. "*What?*"

"They're not lyrics," said Cecil, relighting the roach. "They won't work." He handed me the roach.

I took it, but didn't hit it. "You didn't even look at them all, and you hardly tried."

"I know music. I can tell. Look, could you do me a big favor?"

I nodded, "Sure."

Cecil pointed past me. "Could you leave? And shut the garage door on your way out?"

I felt like my soul had just been torn out of my chest like a hunk of worthless crab grass. I silently handed Cecil back the roach, took my poems, stepped outside into the bright sunlight, reached up, and shut the garage door. As soon as the door swung closed, the rollicking barrel-house piano music started right back up.

Dazedly, I stumbled up Van Ness, yellow papers clutched to my chest, feeling like a squashed bug. I looked down at my poems.

"They can't be *that* bad. It's not possible."

When I got back to 666 I checked my mail, and there was a letter from *Alfred Hitchcock's Mystery Magazine*, in my own handwriting. The envelope was thick, clearly containing a folded-up story. I had read, although he had no personal experience of, that when a magazine accepted a story, the self-addressed stamped envelope that an author must include with every submission would come back *thin*, containing only a check. If it was *fat*, then it contained your story being sent back, and it was a rejection. I opened the envelope and there was my story, "Expectations," with an index card paper-clipped to it. It was a printed rejection slip, in red ink. It had the familiar Hitchcock profile logo, then:

Alfred Hitchcock's Mystery Magazine
229 Park Avenue South
New York, N.Y. 10003

Dear Author:
All manuscripts submitted to this office are read by one or more editors. Their return does not imply criticism of their merit. But they do not meet the immediate needs of Alfred Hitchcock's Mystery Magazine. Although you submitted the enclosed to AHMM, it was also read, for your convenience, as a possibility for Ellery Queen's Mystery Magazine. We hope this meets with your approval and that we will be hearing from you again soon.
The Editors

I shook my head in dismay. "So that means it was rejected by *both* magazines? Great! Even better!"

I went inside.

Opening the bottom drawer of my desk, I dumped in the rejected story, the rejection slip and my poems. I kicked the drawer shut. I turned on my noisy typewriter and lit a cigarette.

I sat at my desk in front of my whirring typewriter, plaintively smoking and staring out the window at Van Ness Avenue, presently jammed with rush-hour traffic.

"Son of a bitch! Just when you think things can't get any worse, they actually can."

I shut off the typewriter and looked out the window.

Cars were parked along both sides of the street. In the unmoving northbound lane of traffic, an LAPD motorcycle cop on a big Moto-Guzzi bike decided he wasn't waiting in traffic anymore. He pulled into the open space between the parked cars and the line of traffic, then gunned it. At that exact moment a Latino man, parked directly in front of me, opened his door to get out of his car.

The huge accelerating motorcycle hit the car door and tore it right off. The cop, the motorcycle, and the car door all continued north for several more car lengths with the car door scratching the hell out of the cars on both sides. When the cop was finally able to stop, he got off his motorcycle and surveyed the damage. Beyond everything else, his motorcycle was completely screwed—the front tire was bent forward right up to the engine. The cop was furious. He stomped over to the bewildered, utterly innocent Latino man who stood beside his doorless car, and began yelling at him.

"*You stupid asshole! Look what you did!*"

The cop grabbed the man, turned him around, slammed him up against his car, and started to frisk him.

Suddenly, people began getting out of their cars all around the incident, saying to the cop, "I saw what happened, it was *your* fault," and "Yeah, I saw it, too, it was *your* fault."

The cop let go of the Latino man and quickly became reasonable. "Okay, all right, let's all just calm down here."

I nodded, "Yeah, let's." I lit up a roach on the end of a hemostat (given to me by Mark, who'd stolen it from the Navy). I took a big hit and blew the smoke out the window, right over the cop's head. If the cop had looked up he'd have seen me in the window smoking dope, but he didn't. He was busy.

While taking a crap at Marvis's house, I found a Time-Life book called *The Alaskan Wilderness* sitting on the back of the toilet. As I leafed through the beautiful photographs of snow-peaked mountains, vast tracts of wooded wilderness, and herds of caribou and moose, it suddenly struck me, "Hey, wait a minute. I'll just hitchhike to Alaska. It's a hell of a lot easier than getting seaman's papers and shipping out to the Orient, yet still so drastic and crazy that no one else would ever consider doing it." It seemed perfect.

I said to Marvis, "What if I hitchhike to Alaska?"

Marvis shrugged, "Sure, why not? You'll have to take the Al-Can Highway, which was built by Negro soldiers during World War II. It's about 2,000 miles of dirt road."

Looking at one of Marvis's many atlases, I traced the route from Los Angeles to Alaska. It was pretty much a straight shot—L.A., San Francisco, Portland, Seattle, Vancouver, then all the way up the large province of British Columbia, then halfway up the enormous Yukon Territory, make a left turn at Whitehorse, Yukon, then 2,000 miles of the Al-Can Highway, and over the border to Alaska. It didn't look so bad. I'd already hitchhiked back and forth from Detroit to L.A. and that was no big deal. So now I'd hitchhike to Alaska. Then I'd legitimately have something to write about, instead of just faking it.

I walked around Hollywood thinking, "I'm outta here. I'm hitch-hiking to Alaska. I'm gone. This place is a memory."

Next to the Francis Howard Goldwyn Hollywood Library on Ivar Avenue was the Ivar Burlesque Theater, an old-time topless club that looked like it had been there forever. As I walked past the tawdry strip club, I stopped to look at the old sign, then glanced down. On the sidewalk directly beneath my feet was the chalk outline of a body with a fresh puddle of blood at the center, exactly where I was standing.

"*Holy shit!*" I exclaimed, jumping about five feet. My sneakers were completely covered with slightly coagulated blood. I immediately became queasy and light-headed, like I was about to pass out. I began rubbing my shoes on the pavement trying to get the blood off.

Around the body outline were three chalk circles with labels saying, "Keys X-7" and "Wallet K-3" and "Glove H-5."

When I got home I scrubbed the remainder of the blood off of my sneakers in the sink. Still, some blood had gotten into the fabric and wouldn't come out.

"Oh, man," I mumbled.

When I stepped out of the bathroom holding my wet shoes, my eyes went straight to the bottom drawer of the desk—to Leigh's unanswered letter.

"What did I do?"

Sherman had a little black plastic 35mm film container full of window pane LSD in his freezer. One lovely warm, sunny day in early June, Sherman and I each took a hit of acid. Once we'd gotten off, we sat around Sherman's place laughing for a solid hour at the concept of "Aerosol Chicken," then we laughed for another hour at the sound of the word, "cheroot," then laughed for yet another hour as we played with Sherman's Sylvester the Cat doll, imitating his line, "*Th*uffering *th*uccotash." By this time our faces ached from laughing so much.

Sherman said, "Hey, let's walk downtown."

"Isn't that kind of far?" I asked.

"Nah! Come on."

"Okay"

Off we went. We walked east along Wilshire Boulevard for miles, past Western Avenue and the old Wiltern Theater, past Vermont Avenue and Korea Town, where there was a strip mall on every corner and all the signs were in Korean. We finally arrived at an office building at the edge of the MacArthur Park. Oddly, the edge of the building's foundation stuck up about 12 feet above the grass.

Sherman said, "Here, let me show you how to parachute jump. This is the perfect place."

I said, "Okay."

Sherman led the way around to the building's entrance. We cut behind the building ending up at the top edge of the jutting foundation, looking down at the grass far, far below.

Sherman explained, "After I served in Vietnam for a year, I tried to re-up for another tour, but they'd already started pulling the Marines out. So I joined the Army Rangers and made 18 parachute jumps over the Everglades. The key to a good parachute jump is—*bend your knees*. When you hit the ground, let your already bent knees bend all the way, like a shock absorber going down, then fall along your side and absorb the impact with your whole body as you roll. Here, watch."

Sherman jumped off. He landed on the grass with bent knees, did a roll and was right back on his feet. No problem, a thing of beauty. Sherman looked up at me. "See. It's easy."

Since I don't like heights to start with, were I not tripping like hell I might very well have been frightened, but luckily I was tripping, so without any hesitation I just jumped off and amazingly did everything right.

I proclaimed, "That was great!"

Sherman said, "And now you'll always know how to take a fall, which is important."

I nodded. "Yeah. Cool. Metaphorical, too."

Sherman looked into my eyes. "How you doin'?"

I grinned. "I'm *sizzling*, how about you?"

"Yeah, *sizzling*. Good word for it."

Sherman and I stretched out on the grass where we'd just been jumping, looking straight up at the tall building jutting up into the blue sky. I lit a cigarette, Sherman lit a cigar. The cigarette tasted great. Sherman's and my smoke swirled upward, commingling, then dissipating into the cosmos.

Sherman mused, "No one's made the definitive Vietnam War movie yet, so I'm going to. I haven't got the story worked out yet, but it's coming to me."

"Yeah, what have you got so far?" I said. "*The Green Berets?* That was crap."

"Oh, boy, was it."

"I did like the song, though. I bought the record."

"Me, too. In the Marine Corps we changed the lyrics." Sherman sang, "If one marine, takes a shit today / He'll wipe his ass, with a green beret."

We both burst out laughing again. We finally had to bury our faces in the grass to make ourselves stop.

Sherman and I wandered around MacArthur Park. We stood in front of a tall brass statue of General Douglas MacArthur, his hands on his hips, aviator glasses, a corncob pipe stuck in the corner of his mouth, looming over dinner plate-sized brass representations of the islands of the Philippines, to which he ultimately did return. Meanwhile, the pond in the park had been drained, and there at the bottom stuck in the mud at odd angles were about 20 old rusty shopping carts.

Sherman and I stared at the shopping carts in awe.

I said, "They were ancient creatures and those are their bones."

Sherman nodded. "Yeah, Shopping Cart-Asaurs,"

"And Shopping Cart-Adons."

We both started laughing hysterically again, then quickly realized that this might be considered inappropriate behavior out in public and might give us away, so we tried as hard as we could to stop, but that meant we had to stop looking at each other, too. We both grabbed hold of our faces to stop ourselves from laughing, but luckily there was nothing conspicuous about that. We staggered around the empty pond in opposite directions, laughing out of control, holding onto our faces while gasping for air.

At some point Sherman and I headed all the way back down Wilshire to the La Brea Tar Pits, another five miles.

Sherman said, "Wanna hear my story about the guy whose life I saved in Vietnam?"

I nodded, "Sure."

"We all went out drinking. When we got back to the base this one guy was lying on his back in his rack—"

"—Rack?" I asked.

"His bed," Sherman continued, "So this guy's so drunk he starts to vomit straight up into his own face." Sherman held up his index finger. "I took my finger and pushed his chin over to the side, so now he was vomiting off the edge of his rack. Had I not done that, he'd have choked to death on his own vomit, so I saved his life."

"Heroic."

"I thought so. He didn't even say thank you."

I blurted out, "I'm gonna hitchhike to Alaska."

Sherman waved his hand dismissively, "You're tripping."

"I am, but I'm still gonna hitchhike to Alaska."

"When?"

"In a couple of weeks."

"Get out."

"No, I am. Seriously."

"*Can* you hitchhike to Alaska? Is it possible?"

"Sure. The one road that goes there is called the Al-Can Highway, it's 2,000 miles of dirt road, and was built by Negro soldiers during World War II."

Sherman seemed impressed. "Wow. Are you kidding?"

"No, I swear."

Sherman smacked me on the back. "Far out."

I grinned, feeling momentarily cool, and slightly macho.

We finally arrived at the La Brea Tar Pits, located right beside the L.A. County Museum. Stepping up to the fence of the big main pit, we stood silently staring down at the occasionally-blooping shiny black tar, decorated with statues of unwitting mastodons stuck in the tar and theoretically sinking, their trunks upraised in panic. The LSD made the scene sort of come to life and seem like it was really happening. Sherman and I watched the frozen scene in drug-induced awe and wonder.

Then a real live bird landed in the black tarry water. Its feathers immediately became coated with tar and, no longer able to spread it wings or fly, it began to drown. Sherman and I looked at each other in wide-eyed horror. We couldn't believe what we were seeing—the fantasy had become reality. No, it wasn't a mastodon, but it certainly was the same idea.

Sherman and I watched the poor bird struggle to stay alive for over an hour. It would go under, then struggle back up to the surface, then go back under again, over and over and over . . . just like the mastodons must have done. However, growing bored, Sherman and I began throwing rocks at the bird, hoping to put it out of its misery, but also for our own amusement. Sadly, though, neither of us was a good enough shot to hit it. When we left, the bird was still going up and down, up and down . . .

Wearily, we returned to Sherman's place. Soon, I decided that I had to go home. Sherman suddenly became very concerned and older brother-like—he was seven years older than me. We had deeply bonded during this acid trip, and now felt like we were close friends.

"You'll be okay driving home?" asked Sherman.

"Yeah," I said.

"You sure?"

"Yeah."

We shook hands, then hugged.

"Be careful."

"I will."

Driving home from Sherman's place, I decided to stay on Sixth Street all the way to Van Ness, thus avoiding the bigger roads. It was a beautiful sunny morning, but for some reason, like possibly LSD in my brain, I was having great difficulty gauging distances. I kept hitting the brake and stopping way the hell before the red lights, then looking all around in panic hoping no one had noticed. I'd then creep forward a few feet, then hit the brake again and panic again.

"Okay. Be cool. Stay calm. No problem," I chanted.

I made the executive decision that I couldn't even be on Sixth Street. I'd have to take even smaller streets. It was only about a mile and half drive, but I ended up taking a long, paranoid, circuitous route.

When I finally pulled up and parked on Van Ness in front of my building I felt like I'd achieved a great victory. All I wanted to do now was to get the hell inside my own apartment.

Once inside I locked the door and immediately stripped naked. I put on *Dark Side of the Moon*, lay down on the bed, still tripping like hell, and valiantly tried not to freak out.

All I kept thinking was, "*Sizzling.*"

"MAY 25, 1977

I went to the movies with Rick and we saw the very first showing anywhere in the world of Star Wars *at the Chinese Theater and it was really a lot of fun. Its story is a bit shallow, and the reasoning for the action wasn't all that good, but the way it was done—wonderful. Now I never need to see another movie like it ever again.*

I bought some of the stuff I'll need for Alaska: flashlight, leather straps, toothbrush holder. I looked at new packs, but decided to stick with my old one. Before purchasing a flashlight I installed two batteries in it to make sure it worked, then was subsequently not charged for them. It's not stealing so I don't feel guilty—as a matter of fact I feel good about it. Something for nothing, it's fabulous.

I also bought a compass, a snake bite kit (containing, among other things, a razor blade and a tourniquet), two spiral notebooks, and four actual Bic pens. I intend to keep a detailed journal along the way. After much consideration I also took the books The End of the Road *by John Barth,* Another Roadside Attraction *by Tom Robbins (both with "road" in the titles), as well as* A Pocket Book of Modern American Short Stories.

MAY 28, 1977

I'm stoned, but not yet smashed. Pink Floyd is playing and it is Saturday night. Yeeha!

I'm leaving for the north country in about two weeks, and I've recently realized that this has been one of the best years in my life. Certainly the best of my adulthood.

Maybe I won't get to Alaska, but I will definitely get to British Columbia, and from there I might go to Detroit. I don't know.

California has been very good to me. I'll really miss this apartment, but a year is more than enough. Must move on, keep going, hut one, hut two, keep going! Hi-ya-hi-ya-hi-ya, hey-oh.

Perhaps another beer?

Oh, most definitely.

I gave Rex notice that I'd be moving out on the 15th of June. Rex looked honestly sad, taking my hand in both of his cologne-drenched hands and shaking it. "You were such a good tenant. You always paid your rent on time. Oh, well." Rex imitated Dorothy from *The Wizard of Oz*, "Everybody comes and goes so quickly around here."

I scrubbed my hand with Ivory soap, but as hard as I tried I still couldn't get Rex's cologne off.

Slowly, one by one, I took down my movie stills and posters. When they were all down it no longer seemed like my place and I began getting sad and nostalgic. "This was a good apartment," I mumbled.

I got all of my belongings together in boxes. Other than my albums and stereo, there really wasn't all that much. I hadn't acquired almost anything in a year: 1,000 used sheets of yellow typing paper, a big yellow ashtray, and that was about it. I stuffed it all into the back of my yellow wagon—everything was yellow. When I was done, I stood in my empty apartment and looked around wistfully.

"Goodbye 666 North Van Ness."

Standing beside my stuffed car, I took one last look at Paramount Pictures. In a year of living directly across the street, I had never once set foot on the studio lot. Maybe now I never would. I saluted the studio.

"Goodbye Paramount Pictures."

I drove over to Marvis's house, picked him up, then the two of us drove out to Santa Monica and had breakfast. We talked for several hours and I thought, "I truly like this guy. He's going to be my friend forever."

Marvis took the wheel and drove us up the Pacific Coast Highway through Malibu. I saw a wide section of shoulder, pointed and said, "That's good right there."

Marvis shook his head and kept on driving. "Uh-uh."

Another wide section of shoulder appeared and I said, "That'll do."

Marvis shook his head again and kept driving. "No."

After a few more minutes, I turned to Marvis and said, "What are you going to do? Drive me all the way to Alaska?"

Marvis finally stopped the car to let me off.

Marvis turned to me and said very sincerely, "Look, I didn't think you were actually going to go through with this."

"Sure, why not? What else have I got to do?"

"Hey, man. It's a *long* fuckin' way."

"I've got all summer."

"Have you told your parents you were doing this?"

"No."

"Why not?"

I rolled my eyes and snorted. "Are you nuts? It wouldn't do them the slightest bit of good knowing."

Marvis looked flummoxed. "Well, what if you get eaten by a bear or something?"

I shrugged, "Yeah, what of it?"

"Well, how will your parents find out?"

"If I get eaten by a bear it won't matter to me how anyone finds out. But it would make a good story. 'Hey, you remember Josh Becker? He got eaten by a grizzly bear in Alaska.' "

"But what about all your shit?"

"If I get eaten by a bear, you can have it."

"Well, be careful, okay?"

"I will. Look after my shit."

"I will."

We shook hands tightly. Marvis wouldn't let go of my hand, grabbing it with his other hand, too, squeezing with the iron grip of a carpenter. I finally pulled my hand back.

"Okay, man. See ya."

Marvis sat quietly watching as I took my backpack out of the car, hauled it over to a good spot on the shoulder of the road, and set it down. As I struggled to get a cigarette lit in the wind, Marvis just sat there in the car, not leaving. Right as I got my cigarette lit, and was about to walk over and ask what was wrong, Marvis pulled a quick U-turn on the Pacific Coast Highway heading back south.

I watched as Marvis drove away down the Pacific Coast Highway in my car loaded with all of my stuff. In a second I lost sight of my yellow wagon among all the other cars traveling up and down the coast road.

I turned to my right and peered out at the vast expanse of the

Pacific Ocean looming endlessly to the horizon. I breathed in the salt air deeply, feeling the bracing ocean breeze on my face. I grinned, feeling good, and finally feeling whole again for the first time in a year.

I took a deep drag on my cigarette, the strong wind whipping the smoke away in spirals. Nicotine burned the bottom of my lungs and I began to cough, deep and hard, until my eyes watered and bright little lights flashed around in my peripheral vision. I stomped my foot, horked up a big loogy, and spat it in the dirt. My whole body tingled for a second. Oh, yeah, I was alive all right, at least for the moment. I blinked several times, took a deep breath, let it out slowly, then grinned.

"Goodbye L.A., where nothing ever happened, and hello adventure!" I plugged the cigarette in the side of my mouth and stuck out my thumb.

Part II:
Going Alaska

As I puffed on my cigarette I thought about the year I'd just spent living in Hollywood, trying to break into the movie business. The closest I'd come to fame and fortune was exchanging a friendly word with Ernest Borgnine, ringing up Farrah Fawcett's pound of sliced turkey, embarrassing myself in front of both Robert DeNiro *and* Robert Wise, and of course, being a prick to Robert Aldrich. I recalled all of the colorful characters I'd met during the year, the funny incidents and silly events, all unspooling in my head like an episode of *This is Your Life*. It all seemed like a distant memory now, even though I'd only moved out of my apartment a couple of hours ago.

I sighed, "Well, I'm glad that's over."

After about 20 minutes of hitchhiking, a white VW microbus pulled over to pick me up. I grabbed my backpack and ran to the bus, thinking, "Shit, this pack's heavy. Too heavy."

Climbing in the side door, I found a Hare Krishna couple in white robes with shaven heads in the two front seats, the woman in the passenger seat holding an infant. In the back of the bus was a guy with a red beard who held tightly onto a backpack similar to mine. Meanwhile, the van was completely plastered with photos of Sri Krishna, literally hundreds of them, with a large photo of a dolphin having a baby at the center of the collage.

I blurted out, "Hare Krishna, Hare Rama."

The man and his wife both smiled warmly, asking, "Are you a follower of Sri Krishna?"

"No," I said, "but I do have the soundtrack to 'Hair.'"

I introduced myself to the Krishna couple, then I sat down beside the guy with the red beard and the backpack. I put out my hand.

"Hi, I'm Josh."

"Alex."

"How far are you going?"

"To Eugene, Oregon. I go to school there at the University of Oregon," said Alex. "How far are you going?"

I grinned, "All the way to Alaska."

This caught everybody's interest, and they all said, "Really?"

Alex asked, "Where did you start from?"

I pointed straight down, "Right here. This is my first ride."

"How long do you think it will take?"

I shrugged. "I don't know. But I've got all summer to get there."

Alex nodded, "Cool. Really cool."

I shrugged, "I hope so."

Alex and I were dropped off just north of Pepperdine College, along the serpentine Pacific Coast Highway. It was a glorious day, and the grounds around Pepperdine appeared shockingly green in contrast with the deep blue sky and the glimmering turquoise ocean.

As we marched along up the road, our thumbs hooked into our pack straps, Alex said, "I'm not sure what to major in."

I said, "You're only in your second semester, you don't have to decide yet. If at all. Many people go all the way through college without figuring out what they want to do."

"Thanks. I'd rather not do that."

"Go into plastics. It's the way of the future."

Alex frowned, "I don't know anything about science."

I shrugged, "I was sort of quoting *The Graduate*."

"Is everything a movie to you?"

"Yes."

"Hmmm."

The next ride was from a fellow with no chin. The chinless fellow had me drive while he studied a speech for school. Alex and I got off in Santa Barbara, then spent the next three hours stuck there, getting acquainted and alternating sticking out our thumbs.

"Just movies?" asked Alex.

"Yep," I said.

"What about theater?"

"It's okay. But I like movies better."

"How do you know?"

"I don't know, I just know. I've always known."

"Huh." Alex seemed perplexed. "You know, there's a Shakespeare festival going on in Ashland, Oregon right now. You wanna go see a play? It's on the way."

I said, "Sure. But I don't have a lot of money, is it cheap?"

Alex shrugged. "Oh, yeah. It's at the university. We might even be able to sneak in."

I nodded. "Cool."

Finally, a black van with British Columbia plates stopped for us. The side door opened and we were hit with a cloud of pot smoke, beer and wine fumes, loud heavy metal music, and yelling.

"Get in, eh, before all the smoke gets out."

The three guys in the van were all long-haired metal-heads in their early 20s from Vancouver, and were all total rowdies, guzzling wine, drinking beer, smoking hash, and blasting Black Sabbath. Alex and I both looked at each other warily, our expressions saying, "Uh-oh, what are we getting into here?" Then we both shrugged and climbed aboard. The door slammed shut. The van burned rubber and swerved back into traffic.

The severely drunk and stoned driver was utterly insane, weaving in and out of traffic at about 90 miles per hour while playing air-guitar with both hands, drinking beer, smoking a cigarette, and steering with his knees while reaching back for the hash pipe.

They offered me and Alex a beer. I took one and Alex declined. They lit another bowl of hash and offered it. I took a hit, but Alex shook his head. The trashed Canadian metal-head rowdy nudged me, confiding loudly, "Your friend, he's a drag, eh?"

I said, "He just had a nervous breakdown and he's on some pretty strong medications, so he probably shouldn't mix his drugs."

The stoners totally understood. "Oh, hey man, that's cool. Totally cool."

Alex glanced at me and smirked.

I said, "But me, on the other hand, I'll take another beer, if you're offering."

They were. "Help yourself, man." They had a 3-foot by 2-foot cooler packed with Labatt's and Molson on ice, as well as several big bottles of cheap red wine.

This madness went on for over a hundred miles.

Finally, when we'd pulled over to the shoulder of the freeway and were all urinating on the side of the road, a cop pulled up. The cop walked around the van to find five guys urinating so much there was absolutely no chance of stopping once we'd started.

The cop said in exasperation, "Oh, for God's sake, fellahs, go find a john or a bush, but you can't water your lizards right here on the road." He then stepped over to the van, opened the side door, and a half a dozen beer cans came clattering out onto the pavement.

The cop shook his head in astonishment. "Oh, man, you gotta be kiddin' me!"

He actually let us off with just a warning, and the absolute assurance that we were headed straight back to British Columbia. These screwballs dropped Alex and I where the Pacific Coast Highway forks to the 101, at San Luis Obispo.

Alex and I ate fish and chips at a quaint old place that Alex knew of. It had been a cheap diner in the 1940s, but now it was a cool fish and chips restaurant, with green, 1950s Bakelite plates and cups. We both had the fish and chips and they were very good. I had a cup of coffee and lit a cigarette.

"So, you don't smoke pot, you don't smoke cigarettes, you don't drink, and I just assume you don't take any other drugs, either, right?"

"Right," said Alex, nodding.

"So what *do* you do?"

"What do you mean?"

"For fun."

"Oh, well . . ." Alex seemed stuck. "You know . . ."

I shook my head. "No, I don't."

Alex shrugged. "I go to the movies . . ."

"Uh-huh."

"And read books, although most of my reading is for school these days. Uh . . . I play pool."

"You got a girlfriend?"

"No, not at the moment."

"When was the last one?"

Alex looked cornered. "Oh, you know, back in high school."

"When you were a senior?"

"No, a junior."

"Did you get laid?"

"Uh, no."

"Are you a virgin?"

Alex was starting to get angry. "Hey! What's the difference? What do you care?"

I blew smoke rings. "Just talkin', man. So, what're you afraid of?"

"What d'ya mean?"

"Well," I said, "you're not *doing* anything. What's up?"

Alex sighed, trying to find the words to explain. "Well, y'see, I just don't want to fuck up, or get into trouble or anything."

"Uh-huh. Why not?"

"Well . . . Fucking up and getting in trouble are bad, right?"

"It depends on how you want to look at it. I've been fucking up and getting into trouble my whole life, but I think it's helped me grow up. I haven't actually accomplished anything yet, but I'm not afraid to try."

"That's you."

"Right."

"That's not me."

"Right again."

"So?"

"So," I said, "I don't even know what I'm talking about. Tell me to shut up and I will."

"No, no, go ahead."

"Hey, I've only known you for one day."

"But . . ."

I shrugged. "But, if someone asked, I'd say, 'Alex is a nice, bright guy who seems afraid of his own shadow.' "

Alex considered this assessment of himself, then nodded. "You're right, I am. I'm afraid of a lot of things, like my parents getting mad at me, or failing a class, or talking to girls, or getting hepatitis from toilet seats, or—"

"—I get it. How'd you get yourself to hitchhike back to school?"

Alex shook his head. "It wasn't easy, and my parents were completely against it."

"But you went anyway."

"Yep."

"Good for you. So, how's it been so far?"

"Great, except for this crazy movie guy I met along the way who won't shut the fuck up."

I grinned. "Sorry."

"It's okay. Honestly, I've had a great time."

"Me, too."

In the restaurant's parking lot, some friendly campers in a pick-up truck gave us a ride to a nearby campground.

> *JUNE 15, 1977*
>
> *I'm sitting in a toilet stall in a campground lavatory in Morro Bay, just north of San Luis Obispo. Today is the first day of my northern adventure, and so far it was pretty good. I made it a long way, too.*
>
> *Alex has gone to sleep, while I, having drunk coffee with my fish dinner, am still awake. I cleansed myself and am now writing this while sitting on a toilet in the campground john.*
>
> *Nighttime is so odd and eerie. It would be difficult spending my first night alone. I'm glad I'm not. Alex knows a goodly amount about movies, so I've been spouting my usual jive. He's been listening, too, and regularly disagrees with me, which makes it much more fun. He's going to Oregon so we may continue traveling together. Perhaps not—we'll see. However a friend made is never really lost, unless of course I just forget him, but now he's on paper, so I won't.*

Anyway. . . Alex and I left Morro Bay and hitched together for the next four days. He turned out to be a wonderfully bright, shy, painfully self-conscious, but very good human being. We proceeded up Pacific Coast Highway 1 and got a ride from a terrifically nice, funny kid named Alex in a red Datsun pickup truck. He kept us stoned and supplied with beer for the next two days.

This Alex was 16 years old and tried to impress us older, bearded guys, with his tapes (Jackson Browne, Dave Mason, George Carlin, etc.) and his dope (which was pretty good), and gave us each a hit of speed. He took us to Berkeley after we stayed the night in Big Sur, ate spaghetti with sardines (too fishy!), and stopped very briefly in San Francisco.

Red-bearded Alex and I were then picked up and taken to Corning, California by a fellow who I believe was named Bill. He had had the bridge of his nose shot off in 'Nam and had tons of war stories about gooks getting shot open like cans of tomatoes; him getting shot at in his patrol boat (PBR) and a bullet coming up through the floor, then through the fat of his stomach and out his cheek (he showed us the scars); and about fucking Vietnamese woman for candy bars and bars of soap, and also having them blow him with his .45 pistol pressed against their head so they wouldn't bite his dick off. He told us about his girlfriend who was a millionaire and bought him an $11,000 van which he wanted to give back because she couldn't buy and possess him. His little girl fell asleep on my lap, causing me to lose feeling in both legs. Then, because I didn't want to disturb her, came pain, followed by agony.

Bill dropped us off in Corning and told us it was the best place to hitchhike in the area. After standing for a half an hour with only two cars going past, we were picked up by a hippie in a V-dub who informed us that Corning was absolutely the *worst* place to hitchhike. Next was a shoe salesman with a kilo of Thai weed that he allowed us to admire, but he wouldn't smoke with us; then a researcher from the University of California, Davis, who was working on a cure for premature births in cattle.

As we were heading out of a little town in northern California, we ran into a kid we had met before in the car with the researcher. He let us have the ramp and he walked up to the freeway. After a bit with no traffic up the ramp, we walked up onto the road, too. All of a sudden a cop coming from the north made a U-turn and nabbed the kid, but didn't see us. Frantically we dashed down the ramp and luckily we were not seen.

After several hours in the dark we were picked up by a hippie couple named Don and Barb who took us to Oregon, where they were from. When we neared their hometown it was 5:00 A.M., so we pulled into a park, tossed our sleeping bags on the lawn, and crashed.

As I lay in my bag on the edge of sleep I could suddenly feel a presence lurking over me. I opened my eyes and two feet from my face was a dark figure with long hair hanging down to within an inch of my nose. This scared me shitless and I gasped. The face pulled back slightly coming into focus and it was Don. He was wearing blue jeans and nothing else.

"Get up," he whispered.

"Huh? What?"

"Barb wants you to come over and fuck her."

"*What?*"

"She wants both of us to fuck her. She likes it. Come on." He started back over to Barb.

"Jesus," I mumbled, not knowing quite what to do next.

Alex glanced over, then pulled his head back into his sleeping bag.

I went over to where Don and Barb were and found her naked on top, with the sleeping bag covering the rest. She was very pretty with long brown hair and a trim body with small firm breasts. Don slid down the sleeping bag revealing her to be entirely nude, ran his hand over her dark pubic hair, then began fondling her breasts. I was still very apprehensive and Barb could obviously sense it. She smiled warmly.

"Don't you have a lot of clothes on?" she said as Don pulled off his pants and climbed into the sleeping bag.

"Enough for three people," I said and disrobed.

Don began having sex with her as she gave me head. When he came, I had sex with her while she gave him head. She climaxed wildly while she was on top of me (which seemed completely arbitrary at that point), and she let out a really high-pitched shriek that not only startled the shit out of me but frightened the birds out of the trees.

At that exact moment a police car drove up.

Don pulled the sleeping bag over all of us and said, "We're gonna get the shaft," then shut his eyes. Barb and I both played dead.

We heard the cop shut his car door, walk over, and speak to Alex who looked over at us with a very dejected expression. The cop came over, turned on his flashlight, and aimed it at us, although it was already light out. There being three of us in the sleeping bag seemed to sincerely puzzle him.

"You can't camp here. It says so on the sign."

Don slowly awoke. "Huh?"

I had my eyes open, but decided not to participate, and Barb continued to play dead.

"Can't camp here," the cop repeated, no longer looking at us, but instead staring out at the lake beyond. "Says so on the sign in front of the park."

"Oh, wow!" said Don, utterly astonished. "We didn't see it. We were all real tired and had to crash. We could hardly see anything; we couldn't even drive anymore."

Oddly enough, the cop looked like he could accept the plausibility of this story, although he still wouldn't look at us. "I could give you a citation . . . but I don't think I will. I'll just give you a warning—this time."

He finally left after a few more exchanges with no comment on the three of us being naked in one sleeping bag.

Barb and Don took us to their hometown of Medford, Oregon where we stopped at a very beautiful place in the woods across a rickety suspension bridge straddling a fast river. I whipped up some bacon and eggs with my butane stove and mess kit, then washed the dishes in the river. I then screwed Barb two more times while she looked at pictures of naked women in *Penthouse* and Don watched us. Alex took a hike.

After that Alex and I decided to backtrack about 20 miles to Ashland for the Shakespeare festival. Along the way we saw the Pioneer Day parade go past in the little town of Jacksonville. It was mainly people riding by on their tractors and lawnmowers.

As we stood there watching the parade, I asked Alex: "Why didn't you fuck Barb? She was cute."

"You think I could have?"

"Yes. Absolutely."

"It would've been weird."

I laughed. "Shit, it *was* weird. It just would've been a little weirder, that's all."

Alex shook his head. "I don't want my first time to be like that."

"With a cute chick who'll let you do anything you want? Okay."

"You think I should've?"

"Sorry. Too late now."

A Streetcar Named Desire was playing in Ashland at the Shakespeare Festival, which I found somewhat incongruous. We were planning on going, but instead we both fell into a deep sleep in the sunshine on the front lawn of the theater. We awoke because the sun had set and it was getting chilly.

We were then picked up by a cute zany chick with a multitude of bracelets and necklaces, driving an old Mustang convertible and blaring Kiss and T. Rex, who took us about 10 miles. Then an absolutely stunning blonde gal named Chris picked us up in a jacked-up Trail Blazer. Alex and I sat in the back with her two boys, Jeff (3½) and Steve (7), both cute, well-behaved little blond kids. Alex and I colored with them while Chris drove and drank one beer after another after another while playing Fleetwood Mac, the Doobie Brothers and Carly Simon. These were obviously her only three tapes.

I snoozed off for a bit and awoke when the car stopped in Eugene, Oregon, the location of the University of Oregon, and Alex's destination. I was half awake and suddenly thrust into an emotional parting scene. Alex and I exchanged addresses, shook hands, hugged, wished each other happy and healthy lives, then off he marched up the road with his pack on his back to whatever his destiny might be. Alex was a good friend for a short time. I hope he gets laid soon.

Beautiful blonde Chris and I then continued north to Seattle where Chris was going to attend her brother's wedding. Both of her children fell asleep, so I moved up to the front seat. Chris and I began talking and I very quickly fell in love with her. She was absolutely stunning: long straight blonde hair (like Peggy Lipton from *Mod Squad*), an absolutely perfect build, and wearing a form-fitting blue sweater, tight jeans, and serious-looking hiking boots with thick red socks poking out the top. Since she kept putting her empty beer cans back in the cooler, then putting the fresh one into a styrofoam holder, I was able to see at a glance that she'd already put away 10 beers. Luckily, she had about 20 more cold ones. She offered me one, and I happily accepted.

She'd started her journey in San Francisco, so I guess between there and Eugene, Oregon was long enough to drink 10 beers. There could have been empties in the cooler when she started, but somehow that didn't seem likely. She began asking me to get her a fresh beer and handing me the empty, and I quickly saw that she was putting away a beer every 30 minutes. We stopped regularly at rest stops, but Chris never stopped pounding them.

I thought, I want to stay up and be with this incredible woman, so I took the hit of speed that young Alex in the red Datsun had given me, and within 10 minutes I fell fast asleep.

I awoke in an hour completely and utterly awake. Chris and I then talked all night long. About me, blah, blah, blah; about her: she loved riding horses, dune-buggying, swimming, driving, and drinking beer. She ultimately drank 20 beers during this drive. She also happened to be an accountant. I talked about books—she had never read any, but she was eager to hear the stories of any I wanted to tell her, so I told her the entire story of Kurt Vonnegut's *Breakfast of Champions*, which just got funnier and funnier the further I went along. Kilgore Trout wading barefoot through a creek of industrial waste that adheres to his feet forming airtight plastic booties that he can't remove that make his feet sweat for the rest of the book got big, big laughs. More beers, another pit stop, the kids slept on, then Chris spoke wearily about her husband and marriage in an exaggeratedly perfunctory tone.

"Matt's a very sweet man, and thoughtful, and considerate, and a very good father . . ." She glanced in the back to make sure the kids were asleep, then she whispered, "But he's so goddamn boring I could just scream! He sells insurance, and I guess he's good at it because he makes a good living, but he doesn't talk about it and I don't ask. He also likes model trains, and so do the boys, and that's nice, right? Not really a fertile subject for discussion, though. Nothing is. So we watch TV and avoid each other." She finished her beer, pulled the empty can from the holder, handed it to me, and asked, "Would you get me another?"

"Sure."

"And have another one yourself."

"Don't mind if I do."

"So," whispered Chris, "you ever take LSD?"

"Yeah," I said. "Quite a few times."

"I've done it five times."

"And?"

"And I'd do it a sixth time, under the right circumstances."

"I tripped a couple of weeks ago. It was incredible. I saw a bird get sucked under the tar at the La Brea Tar Pits."

"What? No. Get out."

"Yeah."

Five beers, three pits stops, and three hours later . . .

Chris said, "Oh, sure, I believe in God, don't you?"

"Well, I don't know. I mean, yeah, but not like any of the religions say it is. I think it's bigger than all that."

Chris nodded thoughtfully. "Yeah, I see what you're saying."

I thought, "I want to fuck you so bad words cannot describe it." My dick had been smushed in my pants for the past million hours, but nevertheless I was totally hard, which she just *had* to know. Except she was married, and her kids were asleep three feet away, so how could it ever work and who was I kidding?

Chris pulled the Trail Blazer into a Denny's right outside Seattle, and said, "Here, let me buy you breakfast."

She woke the kids up and we all had breakfast. She then dropped me off on 85th Street right in the center of Seattle.

It's particularly weird to suddenly find yourself in the middle of a strange large city, dressed like you're on a camping trip, and not exactly knowing where you're going. A middle-aged man going to play golf who had served in north Africa during World War II dropped me off near a bridge. Then two exceptionally ugly American Indians picked me up. They were big and muscular and mean-looking, with scars and fresh bruises and scabs and pimples and blackheads. One of them turned around and said, "Want a beer?"

Even though it was 7:30 in the morning, I eagerly said, "Sure."

The Indian—who looked like he must have recently been in a fight involving bricks and baseball bats—handed me a warm Ranier beer, which I was ever so polite and gracious in accepting and drinking.

Both Indians began speaking their tribal language, pointing back at me, and laughing. I became absolutely certain that they were going to kill me. I then became hyper-aware of the little Buck knife on my belt, my Bar Mitzvah present with my initials on it.

Meanwhile, these two terrifying, beat-up, fucked-up looking Indians dropped me off in Marysville, Washington, with absolutely no ado about anything, and then gave me another warm Ranier beer for the road. Appearances can be deceiving. They lived on the Tulalip Indian Reservation located right there in Marysville.

And there I sat in Marysville, in a misty rain on the edge of the rez, for the next two and a half hours.

An older Canadian couple, who quickly informed me that they were naturalized American citizens, took me to the border of the

U.S.A. and Canada at Sumas, Washington and Huntingdon, British Columbia. I was detained there by a young female immigration official (not bad, I'd've fucked her) who checked and rechecked everything in my past for hours, but never checked my pack. She asked if I'd ever been denied entrance to Canada and I answered no, then began to sweat because I was lying (I had once been turned back at the Canadian border at Buffalo, New York for having a friend's mother's credit card, which he'd lent me, but they didn't believe me and confiscated it, then turned me away) .

Four hours later, after the customs officer's supervisor had grilled me too, I was given a one-week visa. I then lit out across the border into British Columbia, Canada.

After a short ride from an older Canadian couple who were just like the Canadian couple on the other side of the border, I stood for several long hours on a ramp in the hot sun. A sign at the end of the ramp read, "No hitchhiking on freeway. Pickups are illegal."

I edged my way to the end of the ramp feeling hot and paranoid, but got over the paranoia when two different cop cars went by without even slowing down.

Finally, I got picked up by an old guy missing the end of his thumb driving an old pickup truck. He told me about a female bike rider he'd picked up earlier that day who was riding all the way to Mexico. He gave me a can of pop and two cans of fruit juice. He made me promise to write to him from Alaska, so I promised.

The next ride was also in a pickup truck, this time with two big Irish setters in the back. The driver, a chubby, bearded man with long hair, was a teacher of Indian children in a one-room schoolhouse in Clinton, B.C. He asked me if I wanted to smoke some pot, then added, "It's Columbian, not British Columbian." It was very good pot and we both got wasted.

It was raining when I got out, so I ducked into the very buggy woods, and pitched my tent.

In Clinton, B.C., 150 miles north of the U.S. border, and just north of Kamloops, I sat in the pouring rain for five hours. It wasn't cold, and I was wearing my poncho, so it really wasn't that bad. And how often do you actually get to do such a silly thing like sit out in the pouring rain for hours and hours?

If I pulled my head under the poncho I could get a cigarette lit, but then smoking it with my head back out the hole was a bit of a process of keeping my hands cupped around it so it didn't get soaked.

I was finally saved from drowning by some friendly freaks in a beat-up customized van—two boys and a girl, all totally wasted, and thankfully going all the way to Prince George, B.C., about 200 miles north.

"Thank God for friendly freaks," I thought. "Without them hitchhiking would be impossible." They smoked a couple of joints with me, made me several tequila sunrises, and a very pleasant journey was had by all. I never came close to drying out, but after a few drinks and joints it didn't seem to matter all that much.

The sun came out and I walked through the pretty little town of Prince George, situated in a ravine beneath some big sandy hills. I got a ride out of town from a local freak who smoked a joint of some absolutely terrific shit with me, then gave me a pack of little cigars. I got out at the edge of town with my head spinning. I sat down on my pack on the side of the road, in front of a small store, then sat there in that same spot for the next 12 hours . . .

At some point I saw a kid who looked like he was about 11 or 12 wearing shorts and flip-flops go into the store, then come out with a pack of Camels and put one in his mouth. Then he realized he didn't have a light. He glanced over at me sitting on my pack smoking and wandered over.

"Got a light?" asked the kid.

I looked a little surprised. "Aren't you kind of young to be smoking?"

"I'm 14. How old are you?"

"Eighteen."

"Did you smoke when you were 14?"

"Yes."

"Can I have a light?"

"Sure."

I lit the kid's cigarette.

"How long you been sitting here?" asked the kid.

"All day," I said.

"Not much traffic."

"Nope."

"Where you going?"

"Alaska."

The kid nodded. "Long way."

I shrugged. "I guess."

The kid kicked some stones. "How come?"

"Why not? I've got nothing better to do."

"Huh."

I asked, "You like cigars?"

The kid nodded. "Yeah, I do."

I reached into my backpack and took out the pack of little cigars the freak had given me. "Here. I guy gave 'em to me, but I don't smoke cigars."

The kid took them and nodded. "Thanks." He put the cigars in my shirt pocket. "Where do you live?"

I shrugged. "I'm not sure. I lived in L.A. for the last year, but I gave up my apartment. All my shit's in my car at my friend's house."

"So you decided to hitchhike to Alaska?"

"Uh-huh."

The kid thought about this for a while, then asked, "Are you crazy?"

I shrugged again. "Maybe."

The kid nodded. "Sometimes I think I am, then I think everybody else is and I'm the only sane one."

"Right. Me, too."

"Okay, see ya."

"Bye."

"Thanks for the cigars."

"No problem."

The kid said, "Bert," and stuck out his hand.

I said, "Josh," and shook his hand.

Bert walked away up the road, back toward town, then disappeared around a wooded curve.

An hour later I was busily cooking brown rice on my little butane stove when Bert showed back up carrying a small blue and white cooler. He stepped up to me and asked, "Mind if I sit down?"

I waved my hand. "Please. Be my guest."

"What'cha cookin'?"

"Rice."

"Yuk. Wanna beer?"

"Sure. Aren't you a little bit young to be drinking beer?"

Bert opened the cooler, took out two cold cans of Labatt's Blue and handed me one. Bert sat down on the cooler and said, "In northern Canada? Come on."

I took the beer and immediately ran the cold wet can across my hot sticky forehead. "Ah! Thanks a lot."

We both opened the cans, set the pull-tops aside, and touched cans.

"Cheers."

"Yeah. Cheers."

We both drank. I nodded; the beer was good, real good. I set the can down on the side of the road and stirred my rice, now boiling nicely.

Bert pointed. "You really gonna eat that?"

"Yep. Some spices, a little olive oil, it'll be great."

"What do you think you'll find in Alaska?"

I thought, then smiled. "Alaskans."

"Yeah, so?"

"Yeah, so what?"

"Why go to Alaska?"

"Why not?"

"So, you *are* crazy?"

"If going to Alaska for no real good reason makes me crazy, then yeah, I am."

Bert shook his head and sipped his beer. "Huh."

I elaborated. "But I guess I really do have a reason, and that's to have something to write about. I want to be a writer. Like Jack London."

Bert nodded. "Oh, yeah, I get that. That's not no reason, that's a good reason."

"Okay, then I have a reason. To do something that might actually be worth writing about. How's that?"

"That's cool. Sometimes I think about being a writer."

"Yeah?"

"But I haven't written anything yet."

"Well, you better get on it. Fourteen's not *that* young."

"I know. But, hey, I'm stuck here in the middle of nowhere."

I shrugged. "I don't know about that."

"What d'ya mean?"

I paused, took a deep breath, then said, "Well, first I thought I was stuck in Detroit, then I moved to L.A. and I thought I was stuck there, and now here I am stuck in Prince George, British Columbia."

"Yeah?" said Bert. "So?"

"So, you're not stuck anywhere, only in your own head. Or, conversely, you're stuck no matter where you go."

"I don't get it."

"Wherever you go, there you are. I'm still the same guy who was stuck in Detroit, then stuck in L.A., only now I'm stuck here."

Bert sipped his beer and considered this information.

He nodded. "That's heavy."

"Yeah, it is."

Bert and I drank the whole six-pack and talked. I felt kind of worldly and wise, and Bert seemed bright and inquisitive and laughed at all of my jokes. All in all, it was a very enjoyable conversation.

Bert lived in a single-wide trailer with his parents and baby sister in a small trailer park right up the road. Bert took me back to the trailer park with him and showed me an empty spot on the grass where I could set up my tent.

It then rained all night long. By morning my tent was completely soaked through, as was my sleeping bag. I used the trailer park's facilities to shit, shower, and dry all my stuff in a dryer for free.

The next day I sat hitchhiking for 12 hours right in front of the trailer park. Bert came out and visited me a number of times over the course of the day, always bearing some sort of gift, like an ice cream bar or a cup of coffee or a beer, and all gifts were gratefully accepted.

"What if you never get a ride?" asked Bert, seriously.

"I'll move in with you."

Bert laughed. "Right. There's already four of us in a single-wide trailer now. I feel like I live in a submarine. So, have you written anything yet?"

"Yeah. A whole bunch of stuff. A screenplay, over 100 pages of a novel, about 30 short stories, maybe 50 poems."

"Poems?" said Bert, frowning.

I grinned. "You gotta problem with that? You think I'm a fag for writing poetry?"

Bert thought seriously for a second, then nodded. "Yeah. Sort of."

I made a fist. "I can kick your ass, you little wimp."

Bert shrugged. "Yeah? Big deal. I'm 14. Why poetry?"

Puffing out my cheeks, I slowly exhaled. "Well . . . Poetry is generally pretty short, and it's very structured. I feel like I get it, unlike, say, screenplays or novels. The first line rhymes with the second line, the third line rhymes with the fourth, etc. See? Whereas with a novel, it's hundreds of pages long and you can basically do anything you want. So far, that's too much freedom for me, and I don't know what to do with it."

"Too much freedom?"

"Yeah."

Bert turned around wandering slowly back into the trailer park, his head down, clearly in contemplation, occasionally kicking stones.

I grinned. "Cool kid."

After what seemed like eternity, a 1958 Pontiac Strato-Chief stopped to pick me up. I got in. Just as the car was pulling away, I could see Bert walking out to the road holding the little blue cooler. He got to where I had been just in time to glance up and see the Pontiac drive away. In the car's bulbous side-view mirror I could see Bert's diminishing figure just standing there, then in a second he disappeared from view.

"Hi," said the driver of the 1958 Pontiac Strato-Chief. "I'm Alex."

I grinned. "No kidding. You're the third Alex I've met on this trip. I'm Josh."

I looked down and saw that there was no floorboard on the passenger side. I could see the road whizzing past beneath my feet.

Alex pointed, "Be careful of that, eh."

Alex was a friendly 17-year-old with a blond buzz-cut who was going to work on a road crew for the summer in Fort St. John. His dad had gotten him the job because he was still in high school. "I'll be making real adult wages of five dollars an hour, eh, instead of a bullshit dollar-fifty at McDonald's." Alex looked very proud. "Some job, eh?"

"Yeah," I said. "But it'll be hard work."

"That's okay. I don't mind hard work. And I'll save some money.

Then I'll get the fuck outta here, eh. Go to college in Vancouver, or Calgary."

Just then the muffler dropped off the car and went skittering across the road. We stopped and had to wire the muffler back on. Then it fell off two more times.

"Hey, check that out, eh?"

Alex pointed at a very pretty blonde girl hitchhiking. She was dressed entirely in black, with a matching black backpack.

We stopped and the pretty blonde in black got in the back. I turn around and she looked like a little child because of the Pontiac's Strato-Chief's spacious backseat. Her feet barely touched the floor. I said, "Hi, I'm Josh. This is Alex."

She replied, "Layla."

I grinned. "You've got me on my knees, Layla."

She rolled her eyes in boredom and said disdainfully, "That's the first time I've ever heard that. You're very witty."

I was embarrassed and blushed. "Sorry. Uh, don't take this wrong, I'm just curious, but aren't you frightened hitching alone out in the middle of nowhere? I mean, being a girl and all?"

Layla shrugged and replied nonchalantly, "I'm a barmaid in Inuvik, eh, that's way the fuck up in the Northwest Territories on the Arctic circle. All I ever deal with are horny woodsmen and loggers, eh. If I can handle *them*—and I can—you can bet I can handle anything else that ever comes my way, including grizzly bears, eh." Alex and I looked at each other and shrugged—she sounded like she knew what she's talking about.

As we drove along I fantasized that me and Layla finally get dropped off in the same place, are unable to get a ride, then both end up spending the night together in my little tent. In reality, however, I got dropped off on the highway and she was taken into town a few miles away.

I then got a short ride out of Fort St. John from a couple who lived in Windsor, Ontario, located right across the river from Detroit. They were there in Fort St. John visiting relatives. We all spoke fondly of Detroit things, like Cobo Hall and Belle Isle and Tiger Stadium. A nostalgic twinge went off somewhere in my heart, which I noted warily.

I stood on the side of the road outside Fort St. John, British Columbia, 600 miles north of Vancouver, thinking about my old hometown of Detroit. It was a decent, normal place to grow up, I thought. Although since before I could even remember I'd always desperately wanted to go to Hollywood, so on some level I really hadn't paid too much attention to Detroit. But it was a cool place. I knew my way around, and of course all of my relatives and old friends still lived there.

Just saying "I live in Hollywood" always sounded stupid to me, and it inevitably brought on an endless amount of explanation. "Oh, are you in the movie business?" "Oh, are you going to be a movie star?" Always the same kind of bullshit.

But if you said, "I'm from Detroit," people would occasionally respond, "Oh, yeah, where they make the cars." This sometimes led into a discussion of cars, but that was a normal enough topic. Besides, I thought, how could you really develop a sense of individuality living in Hollywood? You're just one more star-struck groupie who gravitated there because it seemed cool.

But by moving to Hollywood you still haven't done anything, you just now live in the same place where they make the movies. So what?

I stood there on the side of the road, just outside Fort St. John, B.C., completely flummoxed by my own life. I lit a Pall Mall, then picked the flecks of tobacco off my lips.

"I don't know where to be. Or who to be. I'm all alone in a God-less universe."

Just then a rust-colored Datsun pickup truck with a small camper on the back pulled over to pick me up. The fellow driving had a bushy red beard and goofy smile.

"Hi," said the guy, "how far ya going?"

I said, "Alaska."

The guy smiled. "Hey, me, too. I can take you all the way. You going to Fairbanks or Anchorage?"

I put my pack in the back of the camper, then got into the cab. "Um, I don't know."

The driver raised his eyebrows. "What do you mean, you don't know?"

"I'm just going to Alaska," I said. "I haven't decided specifically where in Alaska yet."

The guy nodded and shrugged. "Okay. Well, I'm going to Fairbanks. How's that?"

"That's good."

"Then let's go. My name's Tom." He put out his burly, red-freckled, calloused hand. I shook it, and found that Tom was very strong.

"I'm Josh."

"Good to meet you, Josh."

Off we drove north up Highway 97, which was now called the Alaska Highway as it went through the northern half of British Columbia, heading toward the Yukon Territory and Alaska.

Tom pulled a bowling ball-sized black plastic bag from beneath his seat and dropped it in my lap. It was full of stinky, high-quality, bright green marijuana, riddled with little red hairs, with a distinctly skunky aroma.

Tom said, "We have to smoke all of that before crossing the border into Alaska. Are you up to it?"

I shook my head in amazement, my mouth hanging open. "I'm not sure, but I'll certainly give it my best shot."

"Good man." Tom whipped out a stogy the size of a cigar. "Here. Toast this up."

I did as I was told. I took a big hit and closed my eyes. *Oh yeah!* This was the real shit! I tried not to cough and handed the joint back.

Tom took a big hit. "My man in Vancouver laid all that on me. I told him it was too much, but he wouldn't listen to me."

I grinned. "You've picked up just the right hitchhiker to help you with your dilemma."

Tom nodded, "Excellent. Now, what's all this shit about not knowing where you're going in Alaska? Explain."

I took another big hit, held it for a second, then blew it out my nose. With thousands of miles ahead of us, there was absolutely no hurry, so I launched into the totally unexpurgated saga of my life, all leading up to my last year in Hollywood.

" . . . So, everything I've written is bullshit, and I've never made a decent movie. And since I really didn't have anything to write about, I decided to hitchhike to Alaska."

Tom thought about everything he'd just heard. He pulled out a pack of Winstons and offered one to me, which I took. Tom lit both of our cigarettes with a Zippo lighter. He took a puff, then blew the smoke straight up at the ceiling.

"Like Jack London."

"Except he didn't hitchhike."

"Right, he took a dogsled. And built his fire right under a snowy tree."

"Yeah," I nodded. "Bummer."

Tom shrugged. "I think you've done exactly the right thing going to Alaska. It's the greatest place I've ever been. The most intense, that's for sure."

"How so?"

"Well," said Tom, "this'll be my third stint working on the pipeline. It's absolutely great money, but it's *the* hardest job in the world. Well, there's a lot to be said for knowing you're doing the hardest job in the world. If you can cut it, then you really must be made of strong stuff, right? I was working at a pipeline camp near the Arctic Circle where it would regularly get to be 80 to 100 degrees below zero. Everyone would get so tired from working that they literally could not even look up. You'd just shuffle along staring at your feet. Due to this, I physically ran into this guy, *boom*," he clapped his big hands, "and when we looked up at each other we realized that we'd both gone to elementary school together in Wisconsin." Tom and I both laughed. Tom sighed. "Man, they have the world's ugliest hookers at the pipeline camps, and they charge $500! But, I'll tell ya, after a few months, some of 'em really did seem beautiful to me."

I asked, "So you think I should work on the pipeline?"

"Sure. Anything. But if you stay in Alaska for a while, you'll dig it. Honestly."

I explained the $200 to cross the border issue, and that I didn't have much more money than that. And once I crossed into Alaska, I still had to cross back into Canada again, not to mention back into the U.S. yet again after that.

"Work in a cannery in Anchorage. Find some dumbass job in Fairbanks. I'm tellin' ya, man, Alaska is fuckin' incredible, and if you stick around for a while you'll find that out."

I listened, but I wasn't buying it. Stay in Alaska? It certainly was an alternative, and one I hadn't thought of. But it just made no sense.

Meanwhile, Tom and I went on to talk about everything in the world: movies, books, life, religion, philosophy. We sang every song by Simon and Garfunkel, James Taylor, and Crosby, Stills and Nash that we knew, and basically got along tremendously well. All the while trying to burn though this huge bag of stinky skunk weed.

At some point Tom and I stopped on the side of the road tried to get some sleep in the camper on the back of the truck. Unfortunately, these tiny horrible little biting bugs called no-see-ums drove us nuts, so we just kept going.

The next evening we were in Whitehorse, Yukon where we saw both Jack London and Robert W. Service's cabins on Lake La-Barge (where Sam Magee gets cremated in Service's poem, *The Cremation of Sam McGee*). Tom and I had a drink at the Whitehorse Inn where we watched a rock band composed entirely of young native Indians in their late teens wearing blue silk Nehru shirts, unenthusiastically singing Peter Frampton songs. Tom and I both found this highly amusing.

Tom and I drank an extra-large pitcher of dark beer from two oversized mugs. Everything seemed to have a we-don't-shit-around-up-here look and feel to it. After a couple of big mugs we were both sloshed.

Tom said to me, "Look, I don't really give a good goddamn if you stay in Alaska or not, although I personally think it's insane to just turn around and go right back. But anyway, whatever it is you finally end up doing, just don't do it half-assed. The world is loaded with half-assed bullshit, and it doesn't need any more. Whatever you do, take it seriously. Do it the very best you possibly can because, you know what? It *does* matter."

The teen Indian band sang, "Do You Feel Like We Do."

I said to Tom. "You may or may not have noticed in the past million miles, but I'm pretty damn serious about movies."

"I have. And I'm just sayin', don't be half-assed about it, that's all. You get one chance to live your life, and by the time you have the ability to have any understanding of that, you're at least a quarter to a third of the way through it. That's if you're lucky and you don't die young. Then in that next quarter of your life—the quarter I'm presently in—that's when everyone you've ever known buckles under the societal pressure. Do as you're told. Get married, have kids, take a job you don't like. Prepare to retire. But that's your *life*, motherfucker, and you never lived it! So you gotta go for it. Like they say, 'Go for the gusto.' "

Sipping beer from my pitcher-sized mug, I said, "I am. I mean, shit, I'm here in Whitehorse-fucking-Yukon with you right now, right?

Tom nodded, "Right."

"But the point is that I just spent a whole year locked in a room trying to write, and all I came up with was shit. On yellow paper. It's all bullshit."

Tom put his burly strong hand on my shoulder and squeezed it pretty hard.

"Josh. Man. You're 18 fuckin' years old. Of course you haven't done anything that's any good yet—you haven't had time. You will. Stick with it. But go for broke—you've got nothin' to lose." He lifted his mug. We clinked glasses.

"Okay," I said. "I will."

We stopped for the night 100 miles outside of Whitehorse, then continued straight through to Alaska along the Al-Can Highway—which is actually 1,800 miles of dirt road. Along the way the gas stations began getting farther and farther apart until there were 300-mile stretches between them.

The road itself was built up above the level of the surrounding woods, undoubtedly for some sound, weather-oriented reason, but that put the shoulder of the road about five feet below you. Twice along the way Tom and I came upon pickup trucks that had gone off the road, with their tail ends sticking up, one of which was upside down. In both cases we stopped, but found no one in the vehicles.

There were regular runs up and down the road by water trucks spraying water on the road in a futile attempt to keep the dust down. Even still, if there was another vehicle anywhere in front of you, even miles ahead, you were traveling primarily in a dust cloud. You also couldn't be too close behind anyone else anyway because rocks would fly up and break your windshield. Tom ended up with a couple of cracks in his windshield. And meanwhile the Al-Can Highway just went on and on and on . . .

Smoking the 100th or so cigar-sized spliff, I asked . . .

"So, you think there's a God?"

"Yeah," says Tom. "But I think the Eskimos have it right. God's in everything living. Fish. Seals. Walrus. Butterflies. People." Tom pointed at his own chest. "Right here. We're God. Everything is God. Look around. That's all God. In all His glory."

I said, "Wow. Far out."

"God doesn't judge us. God *is* us. You wanna pray to God? Do your very best at anything. Make the very best use of what you have. That's how you honor God. You wanna make movies? Make the best fucking movies you can possibly make."

I nodded. "I will. I mean, I'll try."

"Don't try, do it!"

"I may not get to make any movies at all. They cost millions of dollars and they don't make all that many of them anymore. A lot of people want to make them, but very few get to."

Tom pointed at me. "Then *you* have try *extra* hard."

At one gas station somewhere in the middle of the vast Yukon Territory, there were signs posted all over the place stating, "Free ice cream with fill up," and between the gas pumps was an ancient freezer with a round compressor on top. An extremely old man with a long unruly white beard and dressed in all kinds of rubber rain gear (although it was presently sunny) came out and filled up the truck. He said, "Don't forget about your free ice cream."

After the tank was full and we'd paid, the old man began to walk away. Tom and I both looked at each other, then simultaneously said, "Hey, what about the free ice cream?"

The old man shook his head in astonishment. "Damn, I nearly forgot." He opened the freezer, reached in and handed each of us the smallest ice creams on a stick either one of us had ever seen—the ice cream was literally the size of a matchbox.

As we slowly neared the border to Alaska at Beaver Creek, Yukon, Tom and I both had burning joints in each hand, huffing like madmen, vainly trying to smoke a quarter of a pound of weed in the next 25 miles. We finally stopped a few miles from Beaver Creek, pulled over and dumped about three ounces of beautiful skunk weed into the dirt.

Part III:
Alaska

June 23, 1977.

Tom's rust-colored Datsun pickup truck pulled over and stopped in front of a small, one-room, pre-fabricated building with a sign in front that said, "Alaska Visitor's Information Center and Tok Public Library." Tom and I both sat in silence, plaintively smoking cigarettes, occasionally waving away or swatting at mosquitoes. Finally, Tom said . . .

"So you're just gonna get out here and head back?"

"Yeah," I said. "I made it to Alaska, and that's all I ever meant to do."

Tom sighed. "Oh, man, that's just crazy! I'll take you all the way to Fairbanks, then you can make up your mind there."

"No, I've made up my mind. I'm gonna get out here."

"Why?"

"I don't have enough money to hang around in Fairbanks. Everything's really expensive up here. I've only got $225 left. If I start back now, and don't eat very much, I'll probably be okay."

"But Josh, you hitchhiked all the way up here. It's really fuckin' nuts to just turn around and go right back."

I nodded philosophically. "I guess so, but that's what I'm gonna do."

Tom sighed, then raised an accusing eyebrow. "That's not what Jack London or Robert W. Service would have done."

I sighed. "No, probably not. But they didn't have this $200 minimum rule to deal with, either."

"You could just get a job at a cannery or something."

I guffawed. "Yeah, right. And touch dead fish? You must be completely crazy."

Tom grinned, then shook my hand with a strong, hooked-thumb handshake.

"Okay, man. Good luck."

"Same to you, Tom. It was great meeting you, and it was really terrific hanging out with you for the past few days. And thanks for the ride, and all the smoke, too."

We both put our cigarettes in our mouths, and with our now-free left hands slapped each other on the shoulder.

"My pleasure. It was great hanging with you, too. Be careful."

"I will."

I got out of the truck. I stood up straight and stretched my back. I waved my beat-up blue and white Detroit Tigers baseball cap in front of my face to ward off the mosquito attack. Putting on my hat, I went around to the back of the truck, took out my backpack, slung it over one shoulder, then stepped up to the open driver's window.

"Thanks again," I said.

Tom shook his head in resignation and said, "Be cool," then put the truck in gear and drove off up the road. When Tom's truck got to the junction in the road about a quarter of a mile up, he continued straight, going northwest to Fairbanks, instead of making a left turn and heading south to Anchorage.

For several minutes I stood there watching the truck drive away. It was dwarfed by the distant, though clearly visible, mighty snow-capped mountain peaks looming across the horizon. This was the Alaska Range, the highest mountains in North America, the biggest of which was Mt. McKinley, the tallest mountain in North America, at 20,320 feet.

Eventually, Tom's truck disappeared in the distance below the enormous mountains.

It was now completely quiet except for the chirping birds and the buzzing mosquitoes. There wasn't another car or person to be seen anywhere.

Suddenly, I felt incredibly alone. Cosmically alone.

"What the fuck am I doing here?" I muttered to no one in particular.

I surveyed my surroundings—Tok Junction, Alaska (pronounced "toke"), could hardly be considered a town, consisting entirely of a grocery store, a visitor's information center/public library, a weigh station (with a sign in front stating, "No studded tires May 15 – Sept 1"), a gas station, and two camper-trailer parks, both of which were entirely filled to capacity with Airstream campers.

Since the Summer Solstice had just passed two days before, this far north it now stayed light out for 23 hours a day, with the 24th hour being more gray than black. The sun went around in a big oblong circle in the sky. At this exact moment it could be 4:00 in the afternoon or 4:00 in the morning and you couldn't tell the difference. It was also over 85 degrees, as humid as a sauna, and infested with the most and the largest mosquitoes I'd ever seen in my life. If I stood still for more than a few seconds I was immediately engulfed in a cloud of enormous bloodsucking mosquitoes.

I walked in a circle and lit a filterless Pall Mall. I flicked the match and took a big hit. This was it, Alaska in all its glory. Big mountains and big mosquitoes. So now what was I going to do? Go back? Tom thought that was a really stupid idea, and he seemed like a really bright guy.

I blew smoke rings. I reached up and grabbed a big fat mosquito right out of the air, squashed it, and flicked its dead carcass. There were literally thousands of giant, 2-to-3-inch mosquitoes buzzing all around me, literally creating an audible tone, a ululating ZzzzZzzzZzzz sound. I quickly realized that the reality of the situation was that I was actually inside a vast cloud of mosquitoes. If I just kept moving I was sort of ducking and dodging in and out between them, but the second I stopped moving they smelled me, zeroed in on me, and attacked—thousands of famished, oversized, bloodsucking parasites.

"This is ridiculous." I dodged and ducked, smoked my cigarette, and spoke to myself out loud. I didn't need to hide my craziness at this point, nor was there anyone around to hide it from. "Okay, let's reassess our plan. Move to Hollywood and become a film director, but that didn't work out. Okay, then hitchhike to Alaska to become a better writer, just like Jack London. Uh-huh. And why am I any better of writer now than I was nine days ago in L.A.?"

Hoisting my pack up onto my back, I put my other arm through the second strap, then hiked across the road to the grocery store.

Farren's Grocery Store, the one store in Tok Junction, was a large log cabin with a sign in front that read, "Meat, Prod., Fishing Tackle, Guns, Film & Ice." Guarding the store's entrance were two life-sized cement bears up on their hind legs—one polar, the other grizzly, both clearly marked.

I set my pack down against the grizzly bear and entered the store.

I wandered around inside the store aimlessly for a while, just happy to be away from the bugs. I stopped in front of the candy rack, slowly and carefully selecting a variety of four candy bars which I then took up to the counter.

The tall, bearded, barrel-chested clerk, wearing red suspenders over a blue flannel shirt, appeared stuck on the telephone as he rang up the sale. I paid the two bucks and said, "Thanks."

The clerk smiled and rolled his eyes, indicating that whoever was on the other end of the line wouldn't shut the hell up.

I smiled back in commiseration, took my candy bars and started to leave.

The clerk finally said, "Oh, for Christ's sake, mom, will you just listen for a second . . ."

Outside, I picked up my pack from in front of the angry grizzly bear, slung it over one shoulder and walked up to the road. I dropped my pack on the shoulder of the road, then sat down on top of it. However, after just a few minutes so many mosquitoes had landed on me that I was forced to stand up and walk in circles around my pack, while eating candy bars and waving away the bugs.

After a while a pickup truck pulled out of the visitor's information center across the street heading my way. I slowly stuck out my thumb, smiling in a perky, friendly manner. The truck passed right by. I sat down and in one minute the bugs were swarming all over me again, so I stood back up and continued circling.

A few minutes later I heard the sound of a vehicle approaching from behind. Turning around I saw a pickup truck hauling a mud-spattered Airstream trailer up the road into Tok Junction. The middle-aged male driver of the truck waved to me, and I waved back. Since both camper-trailer parks on either side of the road were already filled to capacity with Airstream trailers, it didn't seem to matter which way he turned. Just a few minutes after that another pickup truck hauling an Airstream arrived, then another, then another . . . I became the unofficial welcoming committee, waving and smiling at each of them as they arrived in Tok Junction after their long journey up the Al-Can Highway.

I paced back and forth and around in circles, a swarm of mosquitoes following me, waiting for me to make a mistake or break my leg or fall asleep so they could swarm in and kill me. I kept shaking my head to keep them out of my hair, and I'd occasionally give myself a good, healthy slap across my own face. After a while I dug through my pack, retrieved a can of U.S. Army surplus bug repellent, sprayed a pool of it into my palm, then wiped it all over my face. For one blessed moment the bugs retreated.

"*Ahhh.*"

I ate three of the candy bars and put the fourth away in my pack for later. I took out my green army surplus canteen and took a swig of water. When I put the canteen away I realized that I had displayed incredible foresight by actually bringing a mosquito head-net with me.

"*Ah-ha!*"

I dug through the pack, found it, put the head-net over my baseball cap, and tied it around my neck. I then put on the gloves I'd also been smart enough to bring. Now I was appropriately dressed for the middle of winter right in the middle of a sweltering hot summer—but at least the bugs weren't biting me!

Lighting up a Pall Mall, I held with my gloves and smoked it right through the net.

I saw a car approaching driving north up the road leading to Anchorage. It stopped at the junction about a quarter of a mile off, let someone out, then the car turned my way. I thrust out my thumb as far as it would go and smiled widely, but the car passed me by. I went momentarily berserk screaming, swearing, and kicking at rocks, then turned and headed back into the grocery store.

I asked the burly clerk, "What's with all the Airstream trailers?"

The guy shrugged his big shoulders. "They're havin' an Airstream convention here. They've been comin' in for three or four days, and there's already gotta be a couple hundred of 'em."

I shook my head. "Wild."

The clerk asked, "Where're you from?"

"Detroit," I said. "But I've been living in Los Angeles for the last year. That's where I started from."

"That's a long way."

"Know any quick ways I can get back there?"

The clerk shook his head and chuckled. "Ain't no quick ways

gettin' to or from Tok Junction. You must know that—you're here."

"But there's like no train or bus or anything out of here, is there? A helicopter?"

"Nope. Quickest way to get to the states would be to drive to Anchorage and catch a flight. How'd ya get here?"

I purchased two more candy bars and a can of Dinty Moore beef stew.

"I hitchhiked."

The clerk nodded, impressed. "Wow. So what're ya doin' here?"

As I took my goods and started to leave he said, "That, sir, is a very good question."

I went back out to where my pack sat on the side of the road. I saw the fellow that had been dropped off a little earlier come staggering towards me from the junction, busily slapping the living shit out of himself. As he got closer I could see that he was completely engulfed in a thick cloud of mosquitoes.

Pulling out my can of army surplus bug spray, I trotted over and handed it to the guy. The fellow truly looked like he was on the verge of insanity, his head jerking oddly and his eyes twitching crazily. He got the cap off the can, then sprayed the bug repellent directly into his face and hair and immediately the bugs begin to disperse. After a few more sprays he handed the can back to me.

The fellow said, "Holy Jesus Christ, thank you very much."

I said, "Sure thing."

"Oh my God, I was about to go insane. I was sure those little suckers were gonna pick me up and take me home for dinner. Really, much obliged."

"Hey, no problem."

Without another word the fellow turned around and headed back from whence he came, about a quarter of a mile up to the junction. I watched him go, then gave myself a spray with the bug repellent and put the can away.

I went back into the grocery store yet again. There was no one else inside and the Clerk was in the midst of clearing the register.

The clerk looked up and saw me. "You still here?"

I groaned. "Two guesses."

"Well, get whatever you're gonna get, I'm closing up."

I picked out one potato, one small onion, then pointed at the meat counter.

"I'll take some of this meat, okay?"

The clerk walked over to the refrigerated meat counter. "Sure. What would you like?"

"How is bison?" I asked.

"It's good. It's just like beef, but a little gamier."

"Okay, I'll take a half a pound."

The clerk wrapped up a half a pound of bison meat in white paper and took it to the cash register. I added several more candy bars to the sale.

"You got a terrific diet there, kid."

"What are you, the dietician of Tok Junction?"

"No, but I eat better'n you do."

I nodded. "So do most people. But seriously, how can you live up here? I've never seen so many mosquitoes in my whole life."

"Well . . . This is the worst month for bugs, though July's not much better. 'Course, usually it's just too damn cold for 'em the rest of the year. So when it's warm enough for there to *be* mosquitoes, then Alaskans are just happy that it ain't cold. See?"

"Yeah, but isn't life rough enough without the worst bugs in the world in the summer and fifty to a hundred below zero in the winter?"

"I guess it is pretty rough, but that's all I know, so I don't have much to compare it with. See, I've lived my whole life in Alaska, born and raised in Fairbanks. But hell, y'know, y'just deal with it. Now I've seen bigger men than me that just couldn't cut it and have to leave, and I've seen smaller men go out in a hundred-below weather in their shirtsleeves, though not for too long, of course. It's all how you look at things, I guess. Half-full, half-empty, that kinda shit, y'know?" He rang up my purchase. "That'll be $4.50." He laughed, "The little speech was free."

"Thanks." I took my bag of stuff and left the store.

I slung my pack on my back and hiked into the woods behind the grocery store. About 25 feet in I came upon a rusty, broken-down, heavy-duty John Deere tractor with a snowplow on the front from the 1960s. About 20 feet farther into the woods was

an even rustier, broken down, International Harvester snowplow from the 1950s. Behind that was another International
Harvester from the '40s, then one from the '30s, then a Ford
snowplow from the '20s, which had mostly rotted away due to
having been made with many wooden parts. There were even
the remnants of yet another older snowplow, also a Ford, possibly a Model T, from the teens, which was now only a rusty
engine block, a frame, and a snowplow, almost entirely grown
back into the soil with tall grass and weeds sprouting right up
through them. This was the Smithsonian Graveyard of snow-
moving vehicles.

Not too much farther into the woods, but no longer visible from
the road or the store, I found a clearing and set up camp. As thousands of mosquitoes took a last stab at trying to kill me, I hastily
erected my fluorescent-orange two-man tent and scrambled inside.
I zipped closed the mosquito netting on the door, then quickly set
about killing every one of the multitude of enormous mosquitoes
that had to their great misfortune gotten in. Once I'd killed about
50 bugs, I collected their dead carcasses together in my palm,
opened the netting two inches, stuck out my hand and dumped
them. I then removed my army coat and head-net. Sighing happily, and finally safe from being devoured, yet no longer having to
roast to death, I then slowly removed my hiking boots. The boots
hadn't been off my feet in several days, not to mention the two
pairs of socks, the outer pair now being dirt-brown mixed with
boot-orange.

"Oh yeah, there we go. *Ahhhhh* . . ."

Getting the boots and socks off my feet felt so good it was erotic, causing me to pop a woody. My feet were deathly white and
wrinkled with a big ugly blister on my left heel. Taking the Buck
knife from my belt, I deftly popped the blister, then squeezed the
juice out onto my dirty sock. Using my bunched up coat as a pillow, I stretched out and relaxed for the first time in over a week. I
closed my eyes, sighing deeply.

Opening my eyes, I shook my fist at the heavens. "I'm still here,
goddamnit!"

After some indeterminate amount of time, I lit a cigarette, then
opened my spiral notebook.

JUNE 23, 1977
I'm sitting in my tent in Alaska. I'm here. I made it. It took nine days.
Uh-huh, so what?
Am I one inch closer to being a film director and writer? No. Am I automatically a good writer now? No. So what the fuck am I doing here?
Must think . . .

So I thought. Then I thought some more. And even more after that. I did the most serious thinking of my life. This too went on for some indeterminate amount of time. It was always light and I had no watch so it was difficult to tell—had it just been 10 minutes, or was it an hour? All I had to gauge the time were the cigarette butts accumulating in the mess kit lid.

Okay, what did I *really* need to do? What specifically did I, Josh Becker, need to do with my life? It clearly wasn't just living in Hollywood since any jerk could do that; all you had to do was move there. Nor, evidently, was it hitchhiking to Alaska, either, although most jerks wouldn't even think of doing such a nutty thing—but still, anyone could. And what do you get once you've done it? You're in Alaska. So fucking what? "It just so happens that I've been to Alaska, and you know what? The mosquitoes are there are *huge.*"

Great.

What I *really* needed to do was to make movies. Deep down at the very core of my being I *knew* I could be a great filmmaker, like Alfred Hitchcock or Stanley Kubrick, if I could just get the chance.

All right, how? Well, Paramount Pictures certainly wasn't going to hire me. Hell, in a whole year of living directly across the street I had never once managed to get past the front gate and step onto the lot. Nor had I tried, either. Perhaps at some point in my future Paramount or Universal or 20th Century Fox might want to finance my films, but there was no reason on earth to believe they would now, or even soon. Seriously, how many 18-year-old directors or writers were there working for Paramount or any of the studios at this very moment? Probably none.

I sighed, blowing smoke into the fluorescent-orange light where it was nearly invisible.

Worse still, I had to honestly admit, even if Charles Bludhorn, head of Gulf & Western, Paramount's parent company, was the next person to pick me up hitchhiking and said, "Yes, I could hire you as a director. What have you got to show me?" I honestly had nothing to offer. What? *The Choice*? *The Case of the Topanga Pearl*? They both sucked. What else did I have? A half-baked screenplay with all of the shots incorrectly written into it. Very impressive!

What the fuck was wrong with me?

I didn't need to go anywhere, like Hollywood or Alaska. I needed to *do* something. Make a movie. Something I could show. With pride, which would then naturally generate more work. If it actually was any good, that is, and I actually had any talent.

Ah, there's the rub. What if I was actually able to make films the way I wanted to make them, or even close to it, and they *still* sucked?

I waved my finger, speaking aloud, "But you can never know *that* until you make them. And it's certainly better to make bad movies than no movies at all."

That seemed true.

"I'd rather be Ed-fucking-Wood than not be a filmmaker."

At some point later in my tent, I had stripped naked and was leisurely smoking a cigarette while scratching my pubic hair. Everything looked exceptionally odd lit by the fluorescent-orange rip-stop nylon tent, and it had to be 90 degrees and about 90 percent humidity. I'd been awake so long and traveled so far that I felt like he was tripping on acid. I began to laugh.

"*Whoa!* I'm in fucking Alaska. How utterly weird."

I began to play with my dick and think about Barb, the hippy chick I'd had sex with numerous times a week ago, but alas, no response. I was just too damn tired to use my imagination.

I said aloud, "Okay, so what's different? I'm not sitting in an apartment in Hollywood playing with my dick—I'm in a tent in Alaska playing with my dick. What's the difference?" I shook my head, then realized I was hungry.

I chopped up the one potato and the one onion, mixed them with the bison meat, added some Worcestershire sauce, salt, pepper, and a dash of olive oil (all of these items were in my pack in little plastic bottles), then I set up my little butane stove and began cooking. It smelled great and as it cooked I realized that I was famished. When it was done, before it even had a chance to cool, I ravenously scarfed the entire thing down— undoubtedly more than a pound of food. I lay there feeling severely bloated and slightly nauseous, but no longer hungry.

"*Grrrrrr . . .*"

A low, throaty growling of something unmistakably inhuman was coming at me from very close by. I peeked out the tent's flap, through the mosquito netting, and no more than three feet away from my face was the face of an enormous wolf, its teeth and fangs bared, saliva drooling from its mouth, growling like it absolutely intended to kill and eat me. I immediately froze with fear. Sweat broke out of every pore all over my naked body. My shaking hand crept to the Buck knife with its tiny six-inch blade, presently covered with chopped onions.

I was going to fight a wolf with a knife? Naked? *Get the fuck out of here!* And meanwhile the wolf kept on growling and drooling, just a couple of inches away. I thought, "What if it alerts the rest of the pack? My chances of fighting one wolf and winning are slim, but I'm dead if the whole wolf pack shows up." It was obviously the smell of the goddamned cooked meat. I had to get rid of it. Hastily, with my hands shaking, I lit a cigarette and blew the smoke all around the tent. When the cigarette was down to burning my fingers, and the wolf was still growling its head off, I lit another one.

This went on for over an hour. The tension and fear were so overwhelming, plus I smoked so many cigarettes in a row, and I'd been awake for so long, that my head began to spin and I finally just passed out.

When I woke up at some unspecified point later—it was still light out—the wolf was gone and my knife was clutched in my hand. I quickly got dressed, pulled down the tent, packed my crap and got the hell out of the woods.

Since I had no watch, I had no idea what time it was. The grocery store and tourist information center were both closed, so I assumed it must be the middle of the night, although it was still as light as mid-day.

I was completely freaked out. I had no idea what to do.

"Fuck! Fuck! Fuck!"

I took back up my position on the side of the road, ostensibly hitchhiking, but all the traffic—which consisted exclusively of vehicles towing Airstream trailers, maybe one every hour or two—was coming from the other direction and stopping in Tok Junction.

Before lowering my head-net, I lit one of my last cigarettes, then smoked it while walking in a wide circle around my pack. If I stopped I would be devoured.

"So," I asked myself aloud, "is that what I'd do if I was in a battle during a war? Fall asleep? Wake me when it's over, fellahs. Fuck! I'm worse than a coward—I'm a narcoleptic."

Meanwhile, since there was absolutely nothing to do in Tok Junction, many middle-aged couples from all over America and Canada, all obviously with a mutual appreciation of Airstream trailers, came wandering over to the one odd, possibly interesting, sight in town—me sitting on my pack on the side of the road wearing a mosquito head-net over my baseball cap, smoking cigarettes, and reading great American short stories.

"Where are you from?" I was asked over and over again.

"I started in L.A., although originally I'm from Detroit," I replied over and over again.

"Did you hitchhike up here?"

"Yep."

"How long did it take you?"

"Nine days. Although I thought it would take at least three weeks."

"Huh. And now you're leaving?"

"Yep."

"Well, good luck."

"Thanks."

Variations of this conversation were repeated at least 20 times over the course of the next nine or ten long, long hours.

The sun went around in its oblong circle in the sky, then every 23 and a half hours or so it would dip behind the tree-line for about a half an hour, everything would get gray, then the sun would pop back up over the trees and a new day would begin 30 minutes after the previous one had ended. It so completely threw off my internal clock that I had no idea when to defecate, so I just didn't.

I wandered into the tourist information center for my seventh cup of free coffee and used their john for the fifth time. Sitting behind the desk all by herself was a heavyset woman wearing a flowered dress. She glanced up at me, smiling pleasantly.

"You still here?"

"I sure am."

"I just made a fresh pot."

"Thank you very much. It's good coffee."

"Thanks. And you can't beat the price, either. I still can't get over the fact that you hitchhiked all the way up here from Los Angeles, got here, and are now turning right around and leaving."

I sighed, "It's really not all that interesting."

"What isn't?"

"See, I guess I was looking for something and I didn't find it."

"Yeah, like what?"

I shrugged. "Wisdom. The point. The reason."

The heavyset woman laughed heartily. "Here in Tok Junction?"

"Not necessarily in Tok Junction, but in Alaska."

"At this time of year all you're gonna find up here is mosquitoes."

I nodded. "Yes, I realize that now. And Airstream trailers."

"Yeah, aren't they cute, all silver with their rounded edges?"

"Yeah. Thanks for the coffee."

"With compliments from the State of Alaska. Have a nice stay. Come back."

"Thanks."

I was seated back on my pack. I brought the coffee up under the head-net to take a drink. I'd smoked all of my cigarettes and was now smoking the butts, holding them carefully between my thumb and index finger. I'd suck the smoke right through the net, then blow the smoke out through the net.

So, should I just start walking east? Or should I just call it quits and die here on the side of the road in Tok Junction? Hmmmm . . . ? Decision, decisions.

Did it seriously and honestly matter at all what I, Josh Becker, did? Ever? Go right, go left, lie down and die. Did it mean anything?

"The only thing in the whole fucking universe with any *real* meaning," said I, "is that which *I* decide has meaning, and that which I honestly believe in. Everything else is bullshit!"

The mosquitoes buzzed, and the wind whistled past.

Yeah? So what?

So, either I was just going to stand there, or I could walk back to the border. It was only about 150 miles, which is nothing up in the vastness of Alaska, but it was still 150 miles of deep wilderness, without any gas stations or anything else, before arriving back at the Canadian border and the tiny town of Beaver Creek, Yukon. Walk 150 miles? It sounded crazy and I couldn't quite convince myself of it.

So I returned to the book I was vainly attempting to read, *A Pocket Book of Modern American Short Stories*, that I'd thankfully brought with me. I'd already finished the other two books I'd brought, *Another Roadside Attraction* by Tom Robbins, that had sounded like it would be a fun traveling book, but turned out to be stupid; and *The End of the Road* by John Barth, which I thought was terrific and found completely captivating. I totally commiserated with the guy in Barth's book who felt so swamped by life's possibilities that he could no longer move. It had turned out that I had a lot more time to read than I had ever imagined due to the tremendous length of time spent sitting in the middle of nowhere waiting for rides, then camping at night all by myself with nothing else to do. Thankfully, the short stories were going very well. So far I'd particularly enjoyed Ernest Hemingway's "The Snows of Kilimanjaro," and Carson McCullers's "A Tree. A Rock. A Cloud." I was presently trying to read "Champion" by Ring Lardner, but sadly I just couldn't concentrate (even though that particular story was the reason I'd bought the collection in the first place, the story being the basis of the 1949 movie *Champion* with Kirk Douglas, a film I really liked).

No cars coming in either direction, the sun going around in a circle, the heat baking, and the mosquitoes swarming.

I suddenly picked up my pack and slung it onto my back.

"Okay," I said out loud. "That's it. It's about 150 miles. If I hump it, going approximately three miles per hour, it should only take about . . . Fifty hours. Two days. Well, big deal." I started walking. I was a tough, mountain man kind of guy, I could handle it. Hell, I hadn't taken a shower or changed clothes in over a week, I'd made it to Alaska, I'd encountered a wolf and lived to tell the tale—I could obviously handle damn near anything, except maybe a career in the movies.

I marched off into the wilderness. As long as I kept moving I didn't even need the head-net. The mosquitoes only became horrible if I stayed still for more than one second and allowed them to find me. This was also good motivation to just keep going all the time. Never stop. Keep marching.

Step by step, up one hill and down another, one long twisting turning mile at a time, I slowly but surely hiked my way out of Alaska. Although I did spend quite a bit of time looking straight down at my hiking boots, I also made sure to look up occasionally. I saw a herd of about 50 caribou that seemed entirely unconcerned if humans like me got near them. They looked up and eyeballed me for a second, but since I didn't appear threatening, they went back to munching grass and ignored me.

As I marched along the road a moose stepped out of the woods about 50 yards ahead of me, then a moment later its calf followed along behind. Well, the calf was as big as me, and the full-grown moose, the mother I supposed, was *enormous*—it had to be 10 feet up to the top of its antlers. I froze and became a pillar of salt, trying not to breathe. The mother moose stared me right in the eye as her baby wandered across the road, her expression clearly saying, "Keep your distance, human, don't make me do something *you'll* regret." I remained frozen. "If I don't move at all, perhaps she'll just forget that I'm here," I thought lamely, with no other plan available. When the calf stepped into the woods on the other side of the road, the big mama moose slowly turned away from me, casually following along after her child.

I took a deep breath, completely shaken. My whole body felt like a limp noodle. As I kept on walking I thought to myself, "Well, at least I didn't fall asleep."

An 18-wheel truck came by going my way so I stuck out my thumb. Incredibly, the truck stopped and I climbed aboard. It seemed like I wouldn't have to walk the entire 150 miles after all.

"How far are you going?" I asked.

"About two miles," the male, middle-aged driver said with a shrug.

"Two miles?" I repeated. "What's in two miles?"

"There's a gas station and a restaurant."

"Really? How about after you eat?"

He shrugged again, "Then I'm going back the way I just came and heading to Fairbanks."

In two miles there was in fact a restaurant and gas station completely in the middle of nowhere that I hadn't even noticed on the way in. As the trucker and I headed inside, the bearded gas station attendant stepped up to a car sitting at the pumps. The car's driver leaned out the window and asked, "You got any bulk oil?"

The attendant shook his head. "Bulk oil? Can't say I do."

"You see I'm losing about a quart of oil every hundred miles," the driver continued, "so I could really use some bulk oil. You sure you haven't got any?"

"Sure's I can be. I could sell you a *case* of oil."

"How much?"

"Well, let's see? Two-fifty a can times 12 cans comes to—"

"—Thirty bucks! *No way!* Where's the next gas station?"

"Tok Junction, 28 miles up the road, but they ain't got no 'bulk oil' neither, and it'll be the same price for a case."

"Yeah, well, we'll see. Where's your air pump?"

"Over there on the back of that pickup, why?"

"'Cause I'd like to use it, if that's okay?"

The attendant sighed and shook his head. "Okay, but you gotta start up the engine on the pump to get it working."

The driver pulled his car up to the pump, got out, and started the engine. As the trucker and I continued inside, the attendant joined us.

"Can you believe that asshole? '*Bulk oil?*' Where the hell does he think he is, Fairbanks? And then after giving me shit he goes and uses my pump and burns up my gas. Jesus fuckin' Christ!" I had a plate of scrambled eggs, toast, and coffee that cost $5. As I paid the cashier, who was also the gas station attendant and the waiter, I said, "Across the street from where I lived in L.A. I could get eggs, toast, coffee, and hash browns, for 89 cents."

The cashier nodded. "Yeah, but it's a long way to go for breakfast."

I checked my money supply and I had $203. I also realized that I was out of cigarettes and couldn't afford to buy anymore.

As I left the café I passed a fellow on his way in smoking a cigarette. I asked, "Hey, mind if I bum a smoke?"

The guy handed me a nearly-full pack of Marlboros. "Here. Take 'em."

"Thanks a lot," I said.

"No problem," said the man. "I quit a month ago. At least, that's what I told my wife."

Standing outside, I lit a cigarette and watched a pick-up truck full of Indians pull up in front of the café. One of the Indians in the back of the truck got out holding a green army surplus backpack and began walking up to the road heading east, the same way I was going. I sped up after him and hollered, "Hey! Wait up."

The Indian fellow stopped, turning to look at me. He was tall and very handsome, with chiseled features, piercing black eyes, and long straight black hair. His face looked extremely tense and he was frowning deeply.

"*What?*" he demanded angrily.

I was totally taken aback by his tone, but proceeded anyway. "Looks like we're both walking in the same direction. Why don't we walk together."

The Indian guy looked me up and down suspiciously, then said informatively, "I'm not walking, man, *I'm* hitchhiking."

I shrugged. "Me, too. Where are you going?"

"Out of Alaska," he stated. "I don't care where the fuck I go as long as it's outta here."

"Where are you from?"

He gave me a withering look and kept walking. "What the fuck do you care?"

I walked along after him, and finally said, "I don't."

"Yeah? Well, I'm from Fairbanks, which is one of the fuckin' places I'm trying to get the fuck away from. This whole fuckin' state eats shit, and that's why I've gotta get outta here!"

We walked along in silence for a while, the last statement sort of just hanging in the humid bug-ridden air. The Indian guy had an enormous, foot-long knife on his belt, a tense crazy look on his face, and he kept bitching under his breath, with only the occasional "fuck" being audible.

Finally, he decided to elaborate. "Man, all anyone's ever done is fuck with me here! I've been fucked around my whole fuckin' life!

It just makes me sick! How far is the border?"

"About 120 miles, I guess."

"We're never gonna get a fuckin' ride, y'know! These fuckin' bastards won't pick up hitchhikers! Alaskans are the worst fuckin' trash that ever lived, and they've fucked with me my whole life!"

As we kept on walking, I finally couldn't help but ask, "What's this all about? Why is everybody fucking with you?"

The Indian stopped, turned around with an absolutely furious expression, looked straight at me and pointed directly into my face. *"Are you fuckin' with me?"*

I shrugged, smiling foolishly. "Nope. Just forget I ever said anything."

We both continued walking in silence. We walked and walked, the sun circling over our heads, Alaska stretching out endlessly in front and behind us, both of us constantly slapping at ourselves to keep the mosquitoes off. Up one hill and down another. After about an hour the Indian stopped, turning to face me in total astonishment.

"You *really* don't know what the problem is, do you?"

I waved my hands. "You haven't told me, so how could I know?"

The Indian shook his head incredulously. "Hold on. Can you actually fuckin' stand there and look at me and tell me you don't know what the problem is?"

I spoke clearly and slowly. "I—don't—know—what—the—problem—is."

The Indian rolled his eyes. "I'm a fuckin' half-breed, can't you see that?"

" . . . No."

"Come on, do I look white to you?"

"No."

"Do I look like an Indian to you?"

"Yes."

The Indian turned and kept walking. "Yeah, well, the fuckin' Indians don't think so. And white people up here can tell the difference, too."

I considered this information as I followed along after him.

We walked along in silence until I said, "By the way, my name's Josh."

He didn't stop or turn around. "Pat."

"Nice to meet you."

Pat slapped his pants pockets and threw his hands in the air. "Man, I don't even know what the fuck happened to my wallet."

"You don't have any money?" I asked.

Pat turned and faced me again. "Hey! I'm no asshole. I don't keep my money in my wallet." I could feel my own wallet in my pocket, with my money in it—was I an asshole for keeping it there? "But," Pat went on, "I don't have any ID."

I shook my head and sighed. Did I really want to go into this? "Look, Pat, god knows I *really* don't want to fuck with you, but without ID they're not going to let you cross the border."

Pat seemed horrified. "What? Why not?"

"This is going to be my third time crossing the border in the last week, so I kind of know what I'm talking about. Without ID and at least $200 they're not gonna let you into Canada."

"Two hundred bucks!" he blurted out. "I haven't got 200 bucks. What the fuck are you tellin' me?"

Pat looked at me like I was his enemy, obviously trying to fuck with him, just like everybody else in Alaska. I suddenly realized that I had just admitted to having at least $200 on me. Was Pat now going to use his enormous knife to take my money?

I went on. "They don't like people walking across the border in the first place—I know, they've fucked with me—but without ID and 200 bucks, forget it."

Pat stomped his foot. "*Oh, man! I've been fucked again!*" He thought for a second, then shrugged. "Aw, fuck it. I'll just sneak across."

I sounded doubtful. "Across an international border? Okay, man, it's your life."

"Then what the fuck do I do?" Pat demanded.

I threw my hands in the air. "Got me."

We kept on walking, and Pat kept proclaiming under his breath, "fuck," then "shit," then "fuck" again, occasionally kicking stones.

We passed a tall fence topped with barbed wire with a sign stating, "U.S. Army Restricted Fuel Testing Center," which seemed extremely out of place in what was honestly and seriously the middle of nowhere.

Pat said flatly, "That's actually a nuclear missile silo."

"Really?"

"Oh, yeah."

"How do you know?"

"I just know. Make any sense to you that there'd be a 'Fuel Testing Center' located right here?"

"No."

"There you go."

I pulled out the pack of Marlboros I'd gotten for free. "Hey, wanna cigarette?

Pat stopped, then nodded. "Sure."

I gave him a cigarette, took one for myself and lit them both with my Zippo lighter. We stopped for a minute and smoked.

"What're you going to do when you get out of Alaska?" I asked.

Pat shook his head. "I don't know. It doesn't matter. I'll figure out something."

I thought, "I'm lucky, I know what I need to do. Make movies. And it *does* matter."

Pat added, "Life sucks!"

I smoked and thought, "I'm sure glad I'm not this poor son of bitch. Life certainly does suck if you think it does."

Pat glanced over at me to see if I agreed with his philosophical assessment of life. I smiled and said, "I got these cigarettes for free. A guy just gave me the whole pack."

Pat said, "Huh," dropped his butt on the ground, stepped on it, and walked away.

I picked up his still-smoldering cigarette butt, squeezed it out between my fingers, stubbed out my own cigarette, put them both in my pocket, then continued along following after Pat.

A little later we saw a beat-up old green Pontiac coming west. As it got nearer Pat stepped over to the other side of the road.

"What're you doing?" I asked.

"I'm gonna hitchhike back to Anchorage and see if I can't catch a flight outta this godforsaken shit-hole."

As the car got closer, Pat stuck out his thumb and the car pulled right over. The engine shut off and out stepped two white, long-haired, thin, slightly crazy-looking guys in their 20s, both with bad teeth. One was tall and the other short.

Pat asked, "You guys goin' to Anchorage?"

"Yep," said the tall one.

The short one said, "Lousy motherfuckers wouldn't let us across the border."

The tall guy said, "The registration on this piece o' shit is expired, can you beat that?" He then opened the trunk, took out a tool-box, removed a Phillips-head screwdriver, went around, and began removing the screws from the car's left taillight. "We never even thought of that. Shit! We drove 700 fuckin' miles for nothin'."

"We're gonna go to Anchorage and see if we can catch a flight."

Pat brightened up for the very first time, actually sort of smiling. "Hey, that's great. Mind if I come along?"

Both guys narrowed their brows, suspiciously looking Pat up and down. It seemed for a second like everything Pat said about Alaska and Alaskans was about to play out in front of me. The two guys looked at each other, then both of them shrugged, the short one saying, "Sure, why not."

Pat and I exchanged a look: my expression saying, "Hey, look, everyone in Alaska isn't an asshole," and Pat's expression saying, "Okay, fine, maybe this one time, but don't fuck with me."

Meanwhile, the tall guy got the taillight lens off, revealing it to be stuffed with tin foil. Within the tin foil was about two ounces of pot. The tall guy grinned maniacally.

"And we get turned back for expired registration, can you beat that?"

We all piled into the Pontiac and huffed down two big fat joints of utterly mediocre weed. When they started the car to begin their journey back west, I got out accompanied by a dense cloud of pot smoke. The tall guy rolled down the window and handed me yet another big fat joint, which I gratefully accepted. I exchanged a look with Pat in the backseat. Pat shrugged and gave me a one-finger salute and sort of a smile. I saluted back and legitimately smiled. Then the Pontiac drove away.

I found myself all alone again, only now I had a big fat joint hanging out of my mouth. I torched it up and kept walking.

I recited Robert W. Service's poem, "The Cremation of Sam Mc-Gee," as I walked. There were about 20 stanzas, and I pretty much knew them all, or at least I once had, and I could sort of fake my way through the others.

There are strange things done in the midnight sun
By the men who moil for gold;
The Arctic trails have their secret tales
That would make your blood run cold;
The Northern Lights have seen queer sights,
But the queerest they ever did see
Was the night on the marge of Lake Lebarge
I cremated Sam McGee

I had a handwritten copy of the poem in my pack, but I didn't feel like stopping and digging it out. And what the hell was a "marge" anyway? As I finished the big joint while I marched along reciting poetry or singing songs, I slowly realized that I had a wicked case of cotton-mouth. I took my canteen off my belt, unscrewed the cap, and to my deep consternation found that it was empty. Bummer! Bad bummer!

As I kept walking, with my mouth somehow getting even drier, I thought about what I had in my pack that was liquid that I could potentially drink—Worcestershire sauce, olive oil, and bug repellent. Nope, none of them would really do. And meanwhile, it would rain hard every hour or two for about 10 or 15 minutes. By the time I stopped, took off my pack, dug out my army poncho, and got it over my head, the rain would have stopped and I would already be soaked. I was so thirsty that I eyed the little mud puddles and considered drinking from them, but couldn't quite bring myself to do it. So I just kept walking and walking and walking, mile after mile, with no cars going either way.

At one point along the way I saw a big black bear leisurely come loping out of the woods about 50 feet in front of me. It was absolutely huge, and so close that I could smell it. It crossed the road and disappeared into the woods on the other side. I didn't even have a chance to react or even stop walking (or fall asleep), although my already dry mouth managed to get even drier.

When I was as severely parched as I'd ever been in my life, and I could no longer find any moisture anywhere in my mouth or throat, and I could hardly breathe, I decided that I would now happily drink from a mud puddle, were there one, but of course

174 | Josh Becker

there wasn't. I stopped, dug through my pack, and found the little plastic bottle of Worcestershire sauce. I unscrewed the cap and took a big slug. *Yow! Nasty!* But it was wet, and now I wasn't desperately thirsty. I kept on walking with the little bottle in my hand, and I soon finished it. I put the bottle away and kept walking.

After a short while I realized that I was now not only thirsty and parched, but I also had the fucked up flavor Worcestershire sauce in my mouth. And I couldn't spit because I had no saliva in my mouth.

"Wow," I hissed. "This is really fucked up."

My next two choices of liquids were olive oil and bug repellent. Well, bug repellent was poison, so that was clearly out of the question. Olive oil, on the other hand, might very well give me the shits, and that would be bad all the way around. For all practical purposes, I was completely out of fluids.

Nothing to do but keep walking. And walking. And walking . . . I watched my hiking boots go up and down, one step after another, and the road seemed endless. I could barely breathe through my mouth, and I didn't seem to be getting enough oxygen through my stuffy nose. Suddenly, the idea of dying didn't seem like all that remote of a possibility. It actually seemed kind of close by, and not all that unappealing, either. Just curl up in a ball on the side of the road, go to sleep, take a nice pleasant nap, and eventually just stop breathing.

Hey! Repellent isn't poison, it's *repellent.* It just stinks, but it probably wouldn't be fatal. But no fuckin' way on the olive oil. Get eaten by a bear, no problem. Die from dehydration, fine. But there was no way in hell I was going to crap myself to death, then have a middle-aged couple hauling an Airstream trailer find me totally covered in my own shit.

Still, olive oil was kind of wet, in its own oily sort of way, and it wasn't poison. I mean, who the fuck was I kidding? Bug repellent was *certainly* poison, just a mild form of it, *and* it really stunk. But olive oil was just a liquid form of a fruit, or a vegetable. Was an olive a fruit or a vegetable? Good question.

My lips were so dry they were cracking. Well, maybe just a little olive oil on my lips . . .

Just then I saw a red flash in my peripheral vision. I stopped. Nothing is naturally that color red. I glanced back . . .

Sitting there on the side of the road, in an environment with absolutely *no* litter of any kind, was a full can of Coca-Cola, sitting upright. I picked it up and it wasn't cold, but it was full, and it was unopened. It wasn't even dirty, or dented. I looked all around to make sure I wasn't on *Candid Camera*. Nope, no camera crew.

I looked up. Was this a sign? I opened the can and took a big drink—*oooh*, warm Coke, very intense, but way the fuck better than Worcestershire sauce! Not to mention olive oil or bug repellent. I could breathe again. I wasn't going to die, at least not at that moment. I took another huge gulp, then poured the remainder into my canteen. I smashed the can, put it in my pack, then kept on walking.

Apparently, fate wasn't quite done with me. Not yet.

It had gotten quite hilly, so when I trudged my way up to the top of a hill I could now see for miles and miles in every direction. Mostly the sun was out and the sky was blue, although I could also see several different storms hovering in the distance, pouring rain onto darkened areas, then quickly blowing past.

As I walked along I realized that I wasn't the least bit frightened, even if a grizzly bear should come running out and eat me. Even should anything happen. Hell, what was the worst that could possibly happen? I could die. Uh-huh. So what? Would it really matter or affect anything at all? No. My existence was utterly and completely meaningless. And should I get eaten by a bear in Alaska, then I'd probably achieve more fame and glory than by just about anything else I could do. "Hey, you remember Josh Becker? He got eaten by a bear in Alaska." "Really? No shit? How cool." However, in lieu of that, I would probably have to *do* something, be it really excellent or particularly awful, to achieve any sort of fame or notoriety.

To *do*. Not just to *be*.

And just being in Hollywood clearly wasn't enough, not by a long shot. They certainly weren't waiting for me. Nobody was waiting for me. I was just one more chump who'd shown up without a plan or anything to show. Just being in Hollywood meant absolutely nothing. Unless I had something to offer, and some way of getting someone, anyone, to listen, I might as well not even be there.

Seeing a lot of movies and knowing a bunch of movie trivia didn't really mean much in the scheme of things, either. There

176 | Josh Becker

would always be the Rick Sandfords of the world who were *way* crazier and more obsessed than I could ever be, who will see more movies, and will always know more trivia. So what?

But writing a good script or making a good movie, well, that was a different story, and that was something I hadn't proven I could do at all. It could still easily turn out that I had no aptitude at all for screenwriting or film direction. So far I'd proven nothing, other than I could find my way to the West Coast, and exist on my own for a year (and manage to get scurvy).

But what I really needed to do was to make some movies and find out if I could actually do what I suspected was lurking within me, which was greatness. Like Alfred Hitchcock or William Wyler. This was something that I had never doubted before, nor truly examined, either. But now, for the first time, my dream seemed like it could very easily be nothing more than mere hubris, the same pipe dream as millions of other Hollywood hopefuls, never to be realized because it was based on nothing concrete. The Lana Turner Syndrome, of believing that all you have to do is be in Hollywood and you will be discovered on the counter stool at Schwab's drugstore. Sadly for me, I didn't have going for me what 17-year-old Lana Turner had going for her.

No, just being in Hollywood meant nothing, unless you're gorgeous, and I wasn't gorgeous. I was a writer and a director, or at least I thought I was, and luckily my looks truly didn't matter. My talent, if I had any, was everything, and how I cared to display it was entirely up to me.

So, the first thing I needed was other people to help me, because you simply can't make movies alone. If you want to make movies, you must have a cast and you need a crew.

My experience trying to make a particularly small, Super 8 movie in L.A. had proven extremely disappointing. However, back in Detroit putting a cast and crew together hadn't really been all that hard because there were all those guys, like Sam and Scott and Bruce, who seemed like they sincerely wanted to make movies, too.

Hmmmm . . . ?

As I kept walking I felt a renewed sense of purpose in my chest. It now seemed like I needed to get back home, to Detroit, and make some movies and try to move on with my life. Hollywood had been a mistake. So was Alaska. Wherever you go, there you are, and I was a prisoner in Josh Beckerville.

I decided right then and there that I would now head back to Detroit and see what was happening, see what those guys were up to, see if it was where I actually felt like I was supposed to be. It hadn't felt like it before, but things were different now. I finally had a little perspective. And besides, I had the whole rest of the summer to kill and nowhere to stay in L.A.

After walking the better part of the next hundred miles, which took at least 24 hours, although it was really impossible to tell, finally a pickup truck filled with an Indian family stopped to pick me up. The cab already had four adults smashed into it, so I got in the back with two Indian kids, both about 11 or 12, one of whom was blind with totally white eyes, the other had withered legs and aluminum crutches. Between the two kids sat a cardboard box stuffed with bags of Doritos, potato chips, popcorn, and cans of Pepsi. The two Indian kids scarfed this shit nonstop for the next 20 miles without ever offering me any, or even speaking a word to me, or to each other. They seemed to be eating as fast as they possibly could, as though it was going to be taken away from them as soon as we stopped.

I swung my legs around and let them dangle off the back edge of the open hatch. I watched the Alaskan wilderness slide away behind me. Soon it would be gone, left behind, and then it would exist only in my memory.

The Indian family in the pickup truck took me to the American side of the border, 20 miles from Canada. They lived in an actual log cabin with pelts drying on racks outside. The four adults got out of the cab and walked up the long rutted path leading to the cabin, leaving the kids to make their own way. The kid with the crutches went first, basically dragging his withered legs, while his blind brother held onto his shirttail with one hand and, clutching the box of junk food with the other, still somehow managed to keep stuffing Doritos into his mouth, too.

I walked for 10 or 12 more miles and saw two cars pass going the other way. A tour bus came driving by going my way, so I stuck out my thumb. I couldn't imagine a tour bus stopping for hitchhiker, but surprisingly it did. The driver opened the door and said, "I can only take you to the border, not across, okay?" I said sure and climbed aboard. Every seat was taken by middle-aged and older white tourists. I stood at the very front of the bus holding onto a pole as we drove away. One of the tourists raised their hand and asked, "Where are you from?"

I said, "I started hitchhiking in Los Angeles, but I'm originally from Detroit."

Another tourist raised their hand. I pointed at them, "Yes?"

"You hitchhiked from Los Angeles to Alaska?"

"Yes, I did."

Another hand went up. "How long did it take?"

"Nine days. Next?"

Someone else asked, "But *why* did you hitchhike from Los Angeles to Alaska?"

I considered the question, and my potential answer. "Well, I guess I needed to get as far away from L.A. as possible, so I could figure out my next move?"

Someone else asked, "So, did you figure it out? What is it?"

I shrugged, "I'm going home to Detroit."

The questioning continued all the way to the U.S./Canadian border at Beaver Creek, Yukon. When the bus stopped to let me off, someone said, "Thank you for your candidness."

I said, "Thank you for your interest, have a nice trip."

I received a polite round of applause, and the bus dropped me off outside the U.S. Customs and Immigration building. U.S. Customs gave me no problems, so I proceeded ever onward to Canadian Customs, where they did stop me, wanting to know where I was going, what was my itinerary, making sure I had at least the required $200 (I had $203), as well as proper ID. Then they just let me pass. These Canadian customs officials were *much* friendlier than the Canadian customs officials had been in British Columbia when I first entered Canada from Washington. Also, my attitude had changed since then. Were they really going to deny me entrance into Canada? Then what would they do with me? Make me live in Alaska? Adopt me? When I was going to Alaska I was afraid; now I wasn't. If the bear or the wolf didn't eat me, the customs officers probably wouldn't, either.

In Beaver Creek I went into a café and had a big breakfast with a lot of coffee. I hadn't slept in several days and had walked most of 150 miles. I also hadn't showered or changed clothes in a week. I was the grubbiest, most bug-bitten, and the most tired I'd ever been in my life, and I felt pretty damn good. I'd gotten to Alaska and I'd gotten back out. And, more than that, at least I was no longer just one more lump of shit sitting in Hollywood waiting for a miracle to happen. I also now had $203 bucks I could blow since I was a U.S. citizen and I was pretty sure that there was no way they could deny me entrance back into my own country.

I left the café holding a large styrofoam cup of coffee and seated myself on the side of the road in front of the Beaver Creek Tourist Information Center. I lit another of my free cigarettes, dug the spiral notebook out of my pack, and wrote:

> JUNE 25, Saturday, 1977
> I'm in Beaver Creek, Yukon, which is the border to Alaska. There is zilch traffic, so I'll probably be here for a while. All I have to do now is get back over the damn Al-Can Highway, eighteen hundred miles of dirt road, which I just crossed a week ago, and everything will be just fine.

I smoked the last free cigarette, stubbing the butt in the pile of eight others. Luckily, I had bought a pack of Pall Malls while the store was still open. It was closed now at 9:00 P.M., and, as always, it was still light out. It hadn't been legitimately dark in over a week, and I was beginning to seriously feel like I was caught in the Twilight Zone, only it was the Daylight Zone.

A big 18-wheel truck drove up from the wrong direction and stopped right across the road from me. The driver rolled down the window and hollered over the loud truck engine, "If you're still here in the morning we'll pick you up." The truck then pulled into the Alas/Kon Lodge across the street and the two truckers went inside. I continued to walk in circles and smoke cigarettes so the mosquitoes wouldn't suck out all of my blood or nest in my hair.

At 1:30 A.M. the same truck drove by going the other way, stopped, and picked me up. I sat in the air-controlled passenger seat while one guy drove and the other guy slept in the sleeper compartment. The truck was a brand-new, very spiffy White Star Western, that they'd christened "Hungery [sic] Eye," which was painted on a clear plastic mud flap on the radiator, so I was able to read the misspelling backward. The cab of the truck reeked of liquor, and both of these guys were completely smash-assed drunk. The driver, Max, a thin, light-haired guy with a growth on the bridge of his nose was from Vancouver. We bounced along the dirt road for about 10 minutes in silence, then Max suddenly hit a button on the dashboard setting off a big hiss of air, causing the truck to jerk to a halt. He hastily opened the door, climbed out of the cab, and vomited on the side of the road. Panting, Max wearily hoisted himself back into the driver's seat, wiped his face, grinned sheepishly, disengaged the air brake with another hiss, then kept on driving. Now it stunk like vomit in the cab, too. I kept a cigarette going and the window open.

We bounced along for a little while longer. Then Max woke up the other guy, Curtis, a thin, bony, pucker-lipped guy from Newfoundland. Max climbed into the sleeper and crashed. Curtis drove along in silence for about 15 or 20 minutes with his head bobbing around like a toy dog in a car window, then he too hit the air-brake, and the truck jerked to a halt. Then he also climbed out of the truck and barfed on the road. Curtis got back in and kept driving, and now it *really, really* stunk of vomit. I lit another cigarette and tried not to breathe while simultaneously trying to keep my gag reflex down. Curtis was so Canadian that he was bordering on Scottish or Irish or possibly gibberish. Every third word was "fuck," every fourth word was "eh," and all he talked about was sex. It was an endless monologue that needed no responses.

"Straight fuckin's for Chinamen, eh. Real men like to eat women out. Really get their fuckin' tongue way the fuck up there, eh. Women love it—it's all they fuckin' care about. And not just their pussies, either, but their fuckin' assholes, too, eh. You gotta get your tongue way the fuck up there, too, eh. That's called felching, y'know, and it's the fuckin' best. I love it. Oh, sure, sometimes there's a clump a shit up there, eh, but that's okay, y'know. And when you stick your tongue way the fuck up there, eh . . ."

This went on for *three entire days*. My only respite was when Max was driving and Curtis was asleep, no doubt dreaming of felching. Also, the way the passenger seat was situated there was no place for me to rest my head. One of the stereo's speakers was directly behind my head so if I started to fall asleep my head would drop back against the speaker's metal edge and it would begin to jackhammer holes into my skull. On top of that, these guys seemed to have only one goddamn eight-track tape, a Freddie Fender album with the song "Wasted Days and Wasted Nights" on it, and they let it play endlessly.

So, with my head lolling around, unable to fall asleep, Freddie Fender blasting in my ear, the edge of the speaker riveting holes in my head, and Curtis in a constant monologue extolling the finer points of sticking his tongue up women's assholes, I sat there for over 72 hours bouncing down an 1800-mile dirt road.

Part IV:

Going Detroit

JUNE 28, Tuesday, 1977 (the very beginning)

Man, was that a long three days!! I'm now sitting beside the road in Cache Creek, British Columbia, at the junction of Highway 97 and Trans-Canada Highway #1 heading east toward Kamloops. It's hot and the bugs are biting, but they are only a minor annoyance compared to what they were in Alaska.

It's now 6:00 AM. Cache Creek, which looks like Texas, is all baked, hilly and scrubby, and is known locally for its overabundance of rattlesnakes. I'm beat and filthy and I stink and I took my last shower about a week ago—good God!

So this is the crossroads right here at Cache Creek. Either I continue south on 97, which is now inexplicably called Trans-Canada #1 west (even though it continues due south for the next 125 miles to Chilliwack), heading back toward Los Angeles; or I begin heading east, on what is also called Trans-Canada #1, but going east, toward Detroit. I chose east. Now I just have to cross most of Canada: British Columbia, Alberta, Saskatchewan, Manitoba, and most of Ontario, to get to Detroit. Only about 2,500 more miles.

I sat there on the side of the road keeping my eyes peeled for rattlesnakes for a couple of hours. I was so tired I began seeing rattlesnakes everywhere. Soon I had myself completely freaked out, in a sweat, with my heart pounding, standing in the middle of the road turning in circles. Another hitchhiker strolled up and positioned himself about 100 feet behind me, which was the proper hitchhiking etiquette. Suddenly, it was like a hammer hit me on the skull and I became so tired I could barely keep my eyes open. "If I pass out here," I thought, "the snakes'll eat me."

Luckily, there was a hotel at the bottom of the ramp, so I immediately decided to go get a room. I was just too dirty and messed up and tired to keep going. Truly six steps after I gave up and started down the ramp, the next car that came by picked up the other hitchhiker. "Well," I thought, "that's how it goes out on the big bad road."

I checked into The Oasis Hotel. After I took a very long shower, then popped the Alaskan water blisters on my feet, I dropped into bed and slept for 11 hours.

> *JUNE 28, Tuesday, 1977 (the night)*
>
> *I'm still wasted. All that sitting in the truck, not to mention all of the walking before it, have completely wiped me out. I have pimples on my ass and legs, and I'm stiff as a board. This R&R is more necessary than I thought. Luckily, I don't have to be out of this room until noon tomorrow. I woke up, glanced at the clock, saw that it was 11:55 and still light out, then I went into a complete panic and was momentarily convinced that I had to vacate the hotel room in five minutes. That was until I realized it was still the same day that I'd checked in.*
>
> *During the long, long truck ride I thought a lot about Detroit, the people back there, and particularly about Renée. In my mind I probably told her to go fuck herself twenty thousand times. I doubt if I'll ever really say it to her, though. I'm having trouble picturing her face, or anybody's, for that matter. That's why it's so easy to tell these people what I think of them in my head, I'm not really seeing them.*
>
> *I now have to defecate for the third time today. I'll be as pure as Ivory Snow when I leave here.*
>
> *When I was nine or ten and wanted to be an actor I set up a deadline for myself in my head—I decided that I had to be a star by the time I'm sixteen years old. Not only did I miss the deadline, but somewhere along the way I stopped wanting to be an actor and switched to wanting to be a writer-director. As I toiled in college after college in Michigan, I told myself that if I could just get to L.A., that*

would be all that it would take—then I'd just shoot to the top as a writer-director. Well, that didn't happen, either.

I'm not necessarily depressed about all of these unmet deadlines and unfulfilled dreams because it is all experience. If I'm going to be a good writer, I need experience, and I guess I've actually had quite a bit of it for my few years of existence. There's just one thing, though—now I don't have a plan or a deadline. I don't know what comes next, not that I knew before, but I thought I did.

I still have my long-range goal of being a director, but now I realize that I haven't got any idea how to become one. Before I always thought I knew, because I never really thought about it. Now I realize how much I don't know, and it frightens the shit out of me.

I spent all day sleeping, then at night I couldn't get to sleep. Instead I watched Monty Python, Room 222, Barney Miller, *and* M*A*S*H. *I ate five candy bars, took a sauna, and jerked-off twice.*

JUNE 28, Tuesday, 1977 (the evening)
I slept for eleven hours and am now wonderfully clean. I'd forgotten that I had soft hair as opposed to dirty, greasy, sweaty, matted hair. Meanwhile, the only movie theater here in Cache Creek is a drive-in. What good does that do me? It's just as well, perhaps, since if when I get to Calgary, Martin Scorsese's new film, New York, New York, *has opened, I am going to go see it. I loved his last three movies,* Mean Streets, Alice Doesn't Live Here Anymore *and* Taxi Driver, *so why wouldn't I love his next film? And he finally has a budget to work with, too.*

It's been thirteen days since I've seen a movie. That's the longest stretch of my life since before I got to Los Angeles in 1976. I'm cleansing my mind, body and soul. It's also putting a little bit of the thrill of going to see a motion picture back into me. The next movie I see, good or bad, will undoubtedly be a lot of fun.

I can presently recall the thrill of sitting in a dimly lit movie theater and waiting for the lights to go down and the film to begin . . .

JULY 1, 1977

It is Dominion Day here in Canada, oh Canada.

I'm now ensconced in a hotel room in Upsala, Ontario, just north of Thunder Bay, and probably less than 20 miles north of Minnesota. Rob, the fellow who picked me up yesterday outside Calgary is asleep in the bed. I'm hiding in the bathroom writing in my notebook.

After I left the Oasis Hotel in Cache Creek, I got eight rides from kindly unknown human beings who weren't traveling very far (between 10 and 40 miles each). One ride was from an old geezer named Ernie in a pickup truck who kept saying, "British Columbia is the most beautiful place in the world. You want beauty, you got it here. You want mountains, you got 'em. Rivers, deserts, valleys, we got those, too. I tell ya, I wouldn't live nowhere else. 'Course I was out on the Atlantic coast in '26, now that was real beauty. Worked on a fishing boat, and boy did we see things there. Beautiful as can be."

As I got out of the truck we finally introduced ourselves. When I told him my name was Becker he said, "Becker? I'll never forget that name. I once spent 22 hours gettin' a guy named Tom Becker out of a caved-in well. First we got his head out, then we lowered rum down to him in a vanilla bottle. We drove a shaft down next to the well, but when Tom come out he was sober as a judge. Twenty-two hours it took."

I hitched for four hours in Revelstoke, B.C., then climbed a small mountain and pitched my tent on top.

The next morning a fellow in a Capri who was on the faculty at Calgary College (or University of Calgary, I can't remember which) on the theater staff, took me to Calgary.

As I walked through the very modern and clean downtown area of Calgary, I drew many looks due to wearing a big backpack, hiking boots and having a beard, I guess. A thin fellow of about 20 wearing a day-pack, shorts and red sneakers sidled up beside me at a street crossing and asked, "Hey, where are you going?"

I said, "To a movie."

This really amused the hell out of him. We walked along together. I got a newspaper and found out where New York, New York *was playing, then he showed me how to get there. He then asked, "Hey, you wanna get high?"*

"Sure, why not?"

"Far the fuck out."

So we stopped at an overgrown vacant lot in the middle of this modern city, and we both sat down on a thick old log. He reached into his pack and pulled out an eight-inch-long brass pipe, then a ping-pong ball-sized wad of tin foil, which he peeled open to reveal a big hunk of blonde hashish. He tore off a chunk, put in the pipe, stoked it up and it was incredibly pungent, sweet and tasty.

Within just a few hits we were both totally stoned. We began to laugh hysterically until we actually fell off the log onto the ground while holding our sides. After about a half hour we smoked some more killer hash, then he went his way I went mine. We'd never even asked each other's names.

Meanwhile, New York, New York *blew. Beautiful photography, gorgeous production design, great cast, some terrific songs, no script at all. None. What a fucking waste! Hey, let's improvise a musical. What a bad idea.*

I hitched out of Calgary.

Rob, the fellow in the bed asleep, while I sit here writing in the bathroom, picked me up outside Calgary, then drove for 30 hours straight without a break (other than fuel). He is utterly and totally emotionless, bordering on catatonic. We haven't exchanged 15 minutes worth of conversation in thirty hours. He has one goddamn fucking 8-track tape—Deep Purple—which he never takes out, turns down or anything. He also has a garbage bag full of beef jerky in the back seat. Every forty-five minutes he says to me, "Hey, could you hand me some of that beef turkey." After the third or fourth time I asked, "Why do you call it turkey? It's called jerky," and he said, "I know, I just like to call it turkey. Hand me some more of that beef turkey." And that's how it's gone all the way across

Canada, the second largest country in the world.

At some point after we passed Sault St. Marie I fell asleep for the 900th time and began having a very vivid dream about that beautiful woman named Chris in the Trail Blazer with the two kids who took me to Seattle. In my dream she and I stopped and made love in the back of her Trail Blazer (luckily, the kids had magically disappeared). I awoke to a very real orgasm. This was only the second wet dream of my life, and the first occurred when I was about eleven. For quite a few seconds I had no idea where I was or what was reality. I looked over at Rob (the robot) and he was staring straight ahead, his face completely expressionless, deadpan, absolutely no hint as to whether or not he had witnessed my writhing climax, while Deep Purple continued to blare out of the speakers, "Smoke on the water / A fire in the sky . . ."

I asked, "Could we stop at a gas station?"

He didn't even look at me. "Sure."

Rob finally dropped me off in Chatham, Ontario, and I wasn't sorry to see him go. I got one more ride to Windsor, then I called my parents from the border. My mom and dad and my little sister Pam came and picked me up. Since we were already downtown, we went for dinner to at one of my parents' favorite places, The Sheik Restaurant, as we had any number of times during my youth.

Part V:

Detroit

After dinner at The Sheik, as we drank coffee, my dad lit a cigarette and asked . . .

"So, what are your plans?"

I took one of my dad's Kents and also lit up.

"Well, actually, I was thinking of moving home."

"Really?" said my mother.

"Yeah, really," I said. "If that's okay?"

My mother nodded, "As long as we establish a few ground rules first."

I nodded, "Okay." Pam and I exchanged a glance. Here it comes . . .

Dad said, "You've got to get a job. Soon."

"Okay."

Mom added, "And no staying up all night watching TV, either."

"Okay."

Mom said, "And we think you should go back to college."

I sighed and shook my head. "No. That I won't do. I've had enough college."

"Then what will you do?" asked dad.

I plaintively puffed on my cigarette, then stated, "I'm going to make movies."

"How?"

"I don't know, I just am."

My dad snorted, flicking his ashes somewhere near the ashtray. "That doesn't sound like much of a plan to me."

"No," I admitted, "but that's what I'm gonna do."

"And work," added mom.

"Yeah, and work."

"And not stay up all night."

"No, I won't."

My dad inhaled deeply, leaned toward me, and said as sincerely as he could, "Josh. Movies are a stupid business. Therefore, anyone who goes into movies must then be stupid. What you don't understand yet is that it doesn't specifically matter *what* you do, just as long as you're successful at it."

I shook my head vigorously. "Uh-uh. No. I don't accept that. It matters to me *very* much what I do, and specifically it happens to be movies."

"And I'm telling you," my dad persisted, "that movies are a stupid business."

"I know, and that only stupid people go into them, like Stanley Kubrick and Alfred Hitchcock, for instance."

My dad sighed. "They were lucky."

"Okay then, I'll just have to be lucky, too."

My dad shook his head forlornly, stubbing out his cigarette.

"Sadly, you can't depend on luck."

I went home to my parents' house, to my old bedroom. Since they'd had my room painted while I was gone, none of my posters were on the walls anymore and it no longer seemed like my bedroom. I began eating indecently, sleeping too much, and hanging out at Howard Johnson's all night long with old friends from high school. I was also ostensibly looking for a job, too.

After waiting what seemed like a reasonable amount of time—a week—I called Renée. Renée's mother answered the phone.

"Hello?"

"Hi, Mrs. Tolken, this is Josh Becker."

"Hello, Josh. Renée's not here. She has her own apartment now in Ypsilanti.

"Oh."

"I hear you drove all the way from Los Angeles to Miami to see her and she didn't even invite you in for a bagel or a cup of coffee."

"Yeah. I mean, no."

"Tell me you didn't drive all that way there *just* to see Renée. You had other things to do, right?"

I nodded, "Oh, sure. I was with a buddy, and I was actually helping him with a business deal. It was just a big coincidence that we were all Miami at the same time."

"That's good. Would you like Renée's number?"

"Sure."

"She's got a new boyfriend, you know."

A dagger went through my heart. "Really?"

"Yes. A bartender. Another *shaygetz*. Randy. Here, let me get her number."

Mrs. Tolken gave me Renée's phone number, and I wrote it down on a scratchpad beside the phone. After I hung up, I stared down at the phone number for a long time. Finally, I tore off the top sheet of paper, crumpled it up and threw it away.

I called up my old buddy Ivan Raimi, my best friend for many years in my youth, who'd grown up around the block from me in Franklin. Ivan was now living in East Lansing and going to Michigan State University. He invited me to come and stay for the weekend. Ivan lived in a big old house full of students, right next to a cool pancake restaurant that had once been a bank, and still had a huge open vault inside.

Anyway, Ivan wasn't there when I arrived, but Ivan's little brother, Sam, and his pal, Scott Spiegel—both of whom had appeared in my film *The Case of the Topanga Pearl*—happened to be there. None of us had seen each other since the film shoot just over a year ago. Sam, Scott, and I found ourselves sitting out on the front porch of the house on a beautiful, sunny afternoon.

Sam asked, "So, how'd the movie turn out?"

I rubbed my face. "Uh, well, not all that great, actually. I needed more shots for it to really cut together properly, and of course I was off in L.A."

"How was L.A.?" asked Scott.

"Big. Daunting," I replied.

"Yeah," said Sam, "movies are just hard to make. I don't feel like I've gotten anything in a movie to work out quite right yet. Or even gotten enough shots to really cut a good sequence, either."

I snorted, "I sure haven't."

The three of us talked about movies for the rest of the day, into the evening, and all night long. At some point during the conversation we went and ate pancakes. We then drove the hour back to Detroit and I watched all of Sam and Scott's movies. I couldn't believe it—they were all pretty damn good. Way better than anything I'd done so far. So, as it turned out, while I was out in Hollywood jerking off and kidding myself, they'd been back in

Michigan making perfectly decent movies. They still hadn't made anything spectacular, but their movies were a whole hell of a lot more functional than mine were. They were at least getting most of the shots they needed to construct their scenes, the sound was clearly understandable, they used stolen, but fitting, music from other movies, silly sound effects, and some of the lighting and special effects were pretty clever, too.

"Shit," I thought. "I know who directed the 1925 version of *Ben-Hur*, and these guys know how to make movies."

Meanwhile, almost all of the films starred Bruce Campbell, whom I knew from way back when in junior high. It turned out that Bruce was both handsome and funny, and sort of the perfect leading man. He played parts as varied as James Bond in *James Bombed*, and Jimmy Hoffa in the aptly titled *The Jimmy Hoffa Story*, doing an absolutely terrific, hysterical job, particularly for an 18-year-old kid.

As the dawn rose, I sat in the back bedroom of the Raimi's house, just around the block from my family's house, watching Super 8 movies with Sam and Scott—and they'd already made quite a few movies at this point, too—I thought to myself, "What the fuck is wrong with me? Am I blind? I'm making movies with these guys from now on. That's all there is to it."

A few days later I phoned Sam who oddly sounded sincerely surprised to hear from me, as though he hadn't heard from me in a year, as opposed to having hung out with me for about 20 hours a few days ago.

"Hey, Josh. What's up?"

"So, you wanna star in my new Super 8 movie I'm going to make called *The Final Round*? It's a boxing comedy."

Sam paused for a long moment, then said, "No, uh-uh, I can't. I'm just about to start shooting my own movie, and I'm starting school, too."

I felt sick to my stomach. "Really? Shit." My plan was going to hell on me immediately.

Sam said, "Oh, by the way, you've got a sound Super 8 camera, right?"

I nodded, "Yeah."

Sam said, "I have a great idea! Why don't *you* come up to MSU with Bruce and Scott on weekends, with your camera, and help *me* make *my* movie? What do you say, *pal?*"

I didn't hesitate. "Sure. Absolutely. But will you take a smaller part in my movie then?"

Sam sighed. "Yeah. Okay. And you're sure you'll show up with your camera, right?"

"Did I say I would?"

"Yeah."

"Then I'll be there—with my camera. I'll bring some lights, too."

Sam said, "Cool. Hey! You know what, you should talk to Bruce. He'll help you make your movie. He's back at his parents' house. He was up at Western for a semester, but then he went psycho and dropped out."

"Really? Okay, sure. What's his number?"

I tried to think of the last time I saw Bruce, and it was probably when I dropped by my old high school, Wylie E. Groves, and found Bruce, who was then a senior, out in the hall building a set for the school play, *The Man Who Came To Dinner*, in which he would star. Since I'd graduated after 10th grade I'd already been in college for two years at that point and felt like hot shit, lighting a cigarette in the school hallway, and making grandiose statements like, "Live theater is dead."

But I'd known Bruce since we were both 10 years old and had just started junior high in seventh grade. Bruce sat behind me in study hall. One day he leaned forward and said to me, "I've got a part in a play."

"What play?" I asked.

"*The King and I*," said Bruce.

"What part have you got?"

"I'm the king's son."

I shook my head sadly. "You should have more ambition and try for the part of the king."

Bruce seemed shocked and sat back in his chair.

A day or two later I was looking through the local newspaper and saw a full-page spread on St. Dunstin's Players, a well-regarded local theater company, and their new production of *The King and I*. There was Bruce in the photo, the only kid entirely surrounded by adults. I felt horribly embarrassed. I thought he was talking about a school play, where he could potentially get the part of the king. But clearly Bruce had so much ambition that he was already in a *real* theater production.

Whoops.

Bruce and I had not only been in several classes together, we'd also been in the drama club together, as well as a school production of Shirley Jackson's play *The Lottery*. I had even cast Bruce as King Creon in my very early silent Super 8 version of *Oedipus Rex* that I'd made for a history class in ninth grade.

Oddly, though, Bruce and I had never actually been friends, just acquaintances.

So I called Bruce's number and his very sweet mother answered the phone. I asked for Bruce, and she said, "One second." A moment later Bruce came on.

"Hello?"

"Hi, Bruce. This Josh Becker. Remember me?"

"Yeah. Live theater is dead, right?"

"Right. I was just talking with Sam, and he suggested that I call you. You see, I have a short script that I think might make a good Super 8 movie. Would you be interested in reading it?"

Bruce said, "Sure, I'll meet you up at Howard Johnson's in an hour."

"You mean, like right now?"

"Yeah."

"Okay."

Howard Johnson's was equidistant from both of our houses. It had been the official hangout of our high school, where you could almost always see people you knew at 3:00 A.M. drinking coffee, smoking cigarettes, and talking. I arrived first, a sheaf of paper-clipped yellow pages in my hand. I had just retyped the script, using the very last of the 1,000 sheets of yellow paper, and it looked pretty good, I thought. I sat in a booth, ordered coffee and lit a cigarette. I felt nervous, like I was on a job interview.

A few minutes later Bruce arrived. I stood and shook his hand. Since I last saw him, when we were both approximately the same size, Bruce had somehow become a much bigger guy, over six feet tall, and rather handsome in a square-jawed, leading man kind of way. As usual, though, he was dressed in a baggy Salvation army suit coat, a white button-up shirt over an undershirt, blue work pants, black lace-up clodhopper shoes, and thick, black-rimmed glasses. Bruce dressed right on the borderline between hip and re-tarded, leaning more toward retarded. Yet even behind the silly outfit, he was clearly now a big good looking guy.

Bruce ordered tea since he didn't drink coffee. He didn't smoke, either.

We quickly got caught up. I'd been to Hollywood, Bruce went off to Western Michigan University and lasted one semester, and now here we both were. We were both 19, and both back at home living with our parents. And, beyond all the rest of the horseshit, we both sincerely wanted to make movies. Real movies. I quickly understood that Bruce wasn't kidding about making movies; he was every bit as serious as I was.

Bruce reached out, put his finger on the yellow script, then pulled it across the table to himself.

"So, this is your new epic, huh?"

"Well, it's an attempt at a comedy," I said. "I saw the films you made with Sam and Scott, which I really liked, and so I tried to come up with my own hilarious version of one those. Something achievable, you know."

Bruce nodded seriously. "Achievable is good." He bent his head down and began reading.

I had imagined that Bruce would take the script home and read it later. But instead he read it right there. I lit another cigarette and nervously smoked it. Bruce slowly turned the page, then the next page, then the next . . . Eighteen pages. There wasn't a single change of expression on his face the entire time. Finally, Bruce turned the last page, looked up and nodded.

"Okay, let's make it."

I was mortified. "But it's a comedy and you didn't laugh once. You didn't even smile."

Bruce smiled now. "It'll be funny when we shoot it."

I was skeptical. "Oh, really?"

"Sure. Absolutely."

I shrugged. "Okay, fine, then let's make it."

Bruce said, "Okay. Now what's the biggest issue?"

"A boxing ring."

"There's gotta be one around somewhere."

"You'd just bet."

"Then we'll find it."

www.ingramcontent.com/pod-product-compliance
Lightning Source LLC
Chambersburg PA
CBHW030929090426
42737CB00007B/371